Red,

Let your fingers do your
traveling for you, as you read
this book.

George & Ruth Morris
1975

The NATIONAL
PARKS of America

The Editors of Country Beautiful • Editorial Direction: Michael P. Dineen
Edited by Robert L. Polley • Managing Editor: Charles R. Fowler
Contributing Editors: Joseph Dever, Frank Sullivan, William Bibber

The NATIONAL

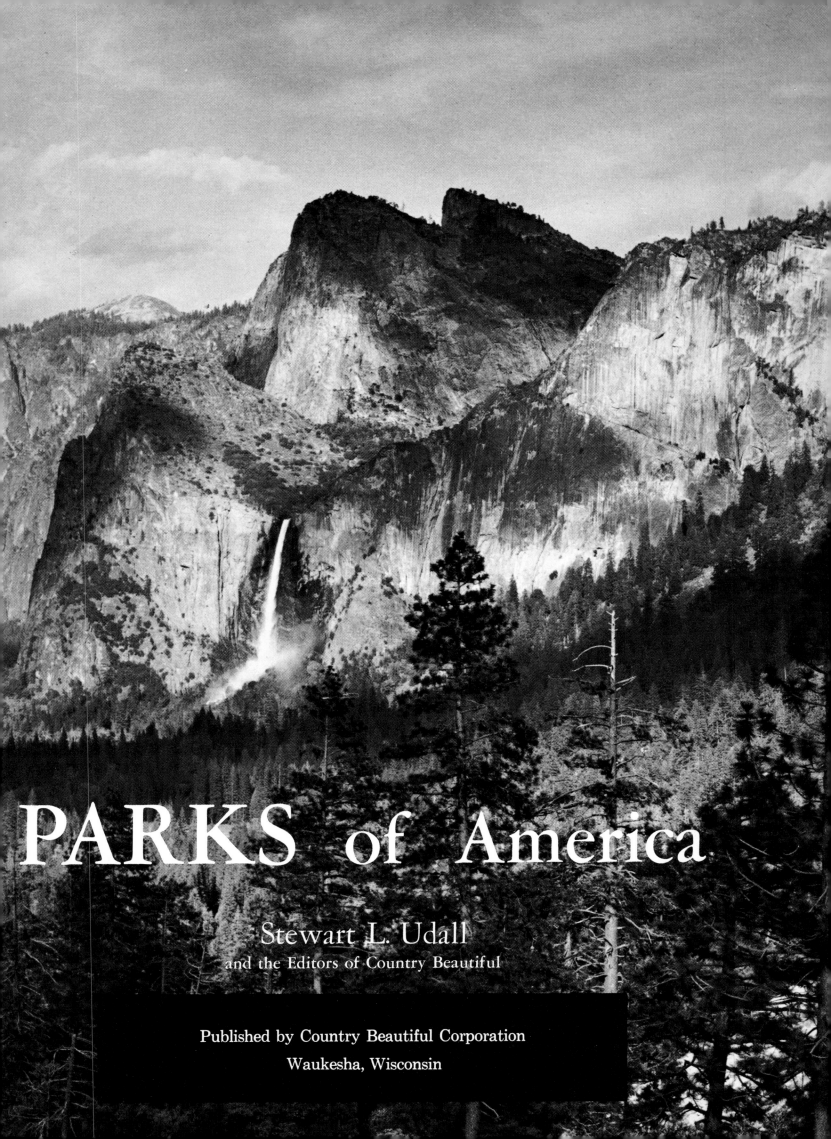

PARKS of America

Stewart L. Udall
and the Editors of Country Beautiful

Published by Country Beautiful Corporation

Waukesha, Wisconsin

COUNTRY BEAUTIFUL: *Publisher and Editorial Director:* Michael B. Dineen; *Executive Editor:* Robert L. Polley; *Managing Editor:* Charles R. Fowler; *Contributing Editors:* Joseph Dever, Frank Sullivan, William Bibber; *Senior Editors:* Kenneth L. Schmitz, James H. Robb.

Country Beautiful Corporation is a wholly owned subsidiary of Flick-Reedy Corporation: *President:* Frank Flick; *Vice President and General Manager:* Michael P. Dineen; *Treasurer and Secretary:* August Caamano.

PHOTO CREDITS

Gene Ahrens, back cover, 59, 60, 62 (bottom), 93 (top), 110, 140 (top), 143, 165 (right), 201 (top), 205 (top); Arkansas Publicity and Parks Commission, 103 (bottom), 102 (Harold Phelps); Ray Atkeson, 219 (top); Erwin A. Bauer, 91 (top), 159, 175 (bottom), 185, 187 (bottom), 196 (top and bottom); Bettmann Archives, 13 (left); Les Blacklock, 226; J. H. Burnett, 126-127; Don Barry Productions (Dennison's Home Films), 200, 201 (bottom), 205 (bottom); Freelance Photographers Guild, 198-199; FPG by Fred H. Ragsdale, 75, 119 (top); FPG by Bob and Ira Spring, 122; FPG by H. Wendler, 134-135, 204-205; Great Smoky Mountains Natural History Association, Inc., 88-89; Arthur Griffin, 19 (all); Bob Gunning, 215, 218 (bottom), 219 (bottom); Grant Heilman, 47, 158-159, 191; Philip Hyde, 223 (top); Howard King, 221; Wallace Kirkland, 44, 51, 52-53, 53; Dirk Lichtenberg from National Audubon Society, 123; Robert J. Mandle, 61 (top right); Phil McCafferty, 82-83; Moulin Studios, Courtesy of Save-the-Redwoods League, 223 (bottom); David Muench, 26-27, 27, 29, 30, 34, 35 (top), 40-41, 41, 46, 49, 50, 54-55, 57, 58-59, 61 (bottom), 64-65, 66, 67, 69, 70-71, 73 (top and bottom), 74, 76-77, 78, 79, 80, 80-81, 90-91, 108-109, 117, 118, 119 (bottom), 120-121, 132 (top), 136, 142, 145 (left), 146, 148, 149 (all), 156-157, 160-161, 166 (bottom), 167, 169 (top), 170-171, 171, 188, 196-197, 206, 207, 208, 210; Josef Muench, 24, 25 (all), 28, 36, 36-37, 39 (right), 42, 43 (bottom), 68, 72, 85, 93 (bottom), 96, 97 (top), 101 (bottom), 111, 120 (top and bottom), 124, 125, 129, 139, 145 (right), 154-155, 163, 164, 165 (left), 168, 169 (bottom), 173, 176-177, 194 (all), 195, 202, 203, 211; National Park Service, 11, 13 (right), 16, 18, 20 (all), 21, 23, 32, 33 (all), 35 (bottom), 38, 39 (left), 45, 48 (top right and bottom), 86, 91 (bottom), 92, 98, 99, 100 (bottom), 100-101, 101 (top), 103 (top), 106, 107 (all), 114 (bottom), 130, 181 (bottom), 186, 212, 224, 225, NPS by Ralph H. Anderson, 174-175; NPS by Jack Boucher, 8, 104-105, 152, 182, 183, 184; NPS by Bryant, 186-187; NPS by Sam Falk, 178; NPS by John M. Kauffmann, 161, 166 (top); NPS by Fred Mang, Jr., 213 (top); NPS by Allen Rinehart, 150, 151 (all); NPS by M. Woodbridge Williams, 48 (top left), 175 (top), 193; Victor B. Scheffer, 130 (top), 131; W. Ray Scott, 105, 112, 113, 114 (top), 115 (all); Bob and Ira Spring, 4-5, 43 (top), 84, 132 (bottom), 133 (all), 140 (bottom), 141, 144 (all), 187 (top), 192 (all), 214-215, 216, 217, 218 (top); Gordon S. Smith from National Audubon Society, 181 (top); David Swanlund, 222 (bottom); Joyce Turvey, 62 (top left), 62 (top), 63; R. Wenkam, 94, 95, 97 (bottom); John Young, 213 (bottom), 222 (top).

Backleaf (full title page): El Capitan (left) and Bridalveil Fall and Cathedral Rocks (right) guard the entrance to beautiful Yosemite Valley and Half Dome (rear center) at Yosemite National Park, California.

CONTENTS

INTRODUCTION 8

MAP OF NATIONAL PARKS 15

Acadia 16

Big Bend 22

Bryce Canyon 26

Canyonlands 30

Carlsbad Caverns 36

Crater Lake 40

Everglades 44

Glacier 54

Grand Canyon 64

Grand Teton 76

Great Smoky Mountains 86

Haleakala 94

Hawaii Volcanoes 98

Hot Springs 102

Isle Royale 104

Lassen Volcanic 108

Mammoth Cave 112

Mesa Verde 116

Mount McKinley 122

Mount Rainier 126

Olympic 136

Petrified Forest 146

Platt 150

Rocky Mountain 152

Sequoia and Kings Canyon 160

Shenandoah and Blue Ridge Parkway 170

Virgin Islands 178

Wind Cave 184

Yellowstone 188

Yosemite 198

Zion 208

Guadalupe Mountains 212

North Cascades 214

Redwood 220

Voyageurs 224

THE BEAUTY AND WONDER OF THE AMERICAN EARTH

The national park idea is a U.S. "original," and today it is being copied by more than fifty countries. This concept is based on two central conservation principles: first, that a country should identify, own outright and preserve for posterity the finest natural wonderlands within its borders; and second, that these natural treasures should be conserved and maintained for the use and enjoyment of the country's citizens (and their guests) under an ecological regimen which will keep them unimpaired for the benefit of present and future generations.

Like many great ideas, the national park concept was not the brainchild of a single individual, and it did not come into existence overnight. Historically, it had its beginnings in 1872 when a small group of congressmen pushed a bill through Congress to set aside a two-million acre wilderness "reserve" in the Yellowstone region of Wyoming and Montana as a permanent "public park or pleasuring ground for benefit and enjoyment of the American people."

The plan for this park originated around a campfire in the territory of Wyoming two years earlier when a party of explorers sat down to contemplate the wonders they had just surveyed. Some of them favored

An aspen grove thrives under summer skies in new Voyageurs National Park, Minnesota.

staking out individual homestead or mining claims on these lands—a step that would have made the Old Faithful geyser the central attraction of a private resort. However, one of the explorers, Cornelius Hedges, was a territorial judge and he argued that the Yellowstone country was so magnificent that it ought to belong to all Americans. This, then, was the kernel of the national park concept that finally prevailed, and Hedge's vision led to the enactment of the 1872 law we celebrate this year as a centennial that marks the launching of the national park movement.

Nevertheless, it is well to remember that by today's standards the role of Yellowstone park in our national life was only dimly understood by its creators. At that time, it was a remote wilderness, and there was no plan for its management or use by U. S. citizens.

During the fifty years following the establishment of Yellowstone park, the modern national park concept gradually evolved. Other than Judge Hedges, the principal "founding fathers" who nurtured this idea to maturity were three men — John Muir, President Theodore Roosevelt and Stephen T. Mather.

Muir's personality combined the attitudes and insights of two pioneer U. S. naturalists, John James Audubon and Henry David Thoreau. On the basis of his experiences in California in the 1880's, Muir became an aggressive advocate of laws to set aside and preserve inviolate the scenic treasures of the country.

Muir wrote crusading articles, harassed legislators, cajoled Presidents—and founded the Sierra Club. Largely as a result of his leadership, the Yellowstone example was magnified, and a string of superb new national parks — Yosemite, Mount Rainier, Crater Lake, Glacier and Mesa Verde — were created.

It was Muir who also exposed the principal flaw in the original national park concept. The final years of his life were dominated by a fight to prevent the building of a dam in the Hetch Hetchy valley within the newly established Yosemite park. He lost this battle, but the bitter controversy he aroused demonstrated that none of the parks were really preserved unless there were laws to prevent invasions by user groups. His fight also underscored the fact that each park needed a conservation-minded superintendent who would fight to protect his lands against all comers.

One of the men who came under Muir's influence was President Theodore Roosevelt. In 1903, they camped out together in Yosemite National Park and Muir expounded his conservation concepts far into the night. Roosevelt, a President who had a feeling for the outdoors matched by few other chief executives, proved to be an apt pupil. In 1906, when Congress passed a seemingly innocuous act giving Presidents the power to sign proclamations creating "national monuments . . . to preserve historic landmarks . . . and other objects of historic or scientific interests," TR had the action weapon he needed. In short order he proclaimed eighteen national monuments in various parts of the U. S., including four—Grand Canyon, Olympic, Lassen and Petrified Forest—which were so majestic Congress later made them national parks. This stroke-of-the-pen statesmanship set a pattern that enabled later Presidents to give park protection to millions of acres of scenic lands in the public domain.

Among those who were inspired by Muir was Stephen Tyng Mather, an energetic Chicago businessman. Recovering in 1904 from a nervous breakdown, Mather turned to the mountains for rejuvenation. He joined the Sierra Club, took part in the organization's annual mountain outings and first met Muir on a camping trip in the summer of 1912. Like Roosevelt and the others, Mather was caught up by Muir's eloquence and enthusiasm.

Two years later, indignant over land depredations in Sequoia and Yosemite and appalled at the sight of cattle grazing inside the parks, Mather wrote an irate letter to Secretary of the Interior Franklin K. Lane, and was promptly invited to join his staff as supervisor of the national parks. Mather accepted this offer in 1915, but at the outset he had very little to work with

in the way of staff or funds since the national parks were then an administrative stepchild within the Interior Department. Each park superintendent was responsible directly to the Secretary of the Interior, who had little time to coordinate the management of the parklands. For many years Muir and his allies had urged the forming of a special agency to administer and protect the parks, and when Mather and Lane championed this idea it resulted in the enactment of the National Park Service Act of 1916. This act created the National Park Service and gave it the clear cut mission to

> . . . conserve the scenery and the historic objects and wildlife therein and to provide for the enjoyment of same in such manner and by such means as will leave them unimpaired for future generations.

Mather thought national parks should be spacious areas of superior scenery preserved forever for the highest forms of outdoor recreation. He persuaded both the Department of the Interior and the Congress to accept this definition, and slowly the country at large caught on to the essentials of our national parks.

Of course, the dilemma that soon plagued Mather and his successors was inherent in the national park concept as defined by Congress. As the most popular parks began to attract thousands of visitors, the problem of "impairment" became a grave one, and each year the National Park Service had to resolve the "use-but-don't-spoil" dilemma. Mather realized that the only solution was to build up a tradition of high standards through a corps of highly trained, dedicated personnel, who would make sound judgments on day to day issues with one eye always on the future. As a result of this commitment, the National Park Service today exemplifies one of the highest traditions of public service.

When Mather took office in 1915, there were fourteen maladministered national parks. By the time failing health forced him to resign in 1929, there were twenty-one units under one creative plan of management.

More and more Americans see, as Muir did, that in this increasingly commercial civilization there must be natural sanctuaries where commercialism is barred, where factories, subdivisions, billboards, power plants, dams and all forms of economic use are completely and permanently prohibited—and where every man may enjoy the spiritual exhilaration of untrammeled landscapes. Americans have belatedly begun to prize the values of their wild lands and parklands, and each year more of them understand the significance of John Muir's good counsel:

Climb the mountains and get their good tidings, Nature's peace will flow into you as sunshine flows into trees. The winds will blow their own freshness into you and the storms their energy, while cares will drop off like autumn leaves.

In the 1960's, during my eight years as Secretary of the Interior, new problems and new ecological insights caused us to recognize the impact of activities which were to that time considered "outside" the parks. For example, when a sonic boom from a military plane collapsed a fragile Indian ruin in a southwestern park, we knew we had to enter the fight against the SST. When evidence accumulated that the widespread use of DDT and other hard pesticides was destroying the reproductive capacities of eagles, ospreys and other birds, we realized we had to take sides with Rachel Carson in the fight against long-lived poisons. And when small streams in the urbanized areas of Yellowstone and Yosemite were polluted, we realized that a process of "deurbanizing" these areas had to begin.

George B. Hartzog, Director, National Park Service.

By 1972, our system of national parks has become truly national. It now embraces thirty million acres (or 1.3% of the total U. S. land mass) and contains representative landforms of all major regions. Today there are 284 separate units of the National Park System, including 74 natural areas, 172 historical areas and 38 recreational areas. Delaware and Connecticut are the only states with no land under National Park Service protection.

However, the thirty-seven true national parks are rightly considered the centerpieces of the system. They include some of the world's most beautiful and majestic gorges, forests, seashores, reefs, mountains, canyons, caverns, islands, glaciers, volcanoes, craters, deserts and swamps. Geographically, they extend from Mauna Loa in Hawaii to Alaska's Mt. McKinley, from the rocky islands of eastern Maine to the remarkable living reefs of the Virgin Islands, from Florida's Everglades to the huge park that hugs the Mexican border at Big Bend in Texas.

The national parks play an important role in our national life. They give refreshing outdoor experiences to millions of Americans; they serve as wilderness laboratories for scientists and they are outdoor classrooms for Americans of all ages who want to understand the natural world. Most important, they have helped make the wilderness ethic—with its inherent skepticism of mechanized "progress"—part of our national creed.

But these contributions notwithstanding, the Yellowstone centenary finds our parklands in serious trouble today. Ecologists have warned that no park, however remote, is an island which can wholly escape the impacts of modern man and his machines. Rivers and winds and ocean tides carry pollutants and poisons everywhere. In the long run even these protected enclaves will be slowly impaired unless the planetary environmental crisis is resolved. Faced by this reality, in recent years most U. S. conservationists have begun to think globally and get involved in the big fight to save the entire earth.

The immediate crisis, however, centers on the most visited and most accessible parks, such as the Great Smokies, Yellowstone, Yosemite, the Everglades and Grand Canyon. Its causes include overuse pressures from a growing, increasingly mobile population; the parklands are finite, and as long as more people—transported in more machines—want to "enjoy" them, the park managers are faced with demands difficult to reconcile with their preservation goals.

The overdevelopment of some parks—too many roads, hotels and mass facilities catering to automobile visitors — has compounded this problem. Until recent years, the National Park Service measured its success by the number of visitors who checked-in at the front gate each year. This shallow game of "crowdmanship" distorted the purpose of the parks. And it has also led to misguided policies that put greater emphasis on "from-the-car" park viewing than on those intimate outdoor experiences that should be the essence of a visit to our national parks.

Already, the park service has recognized that it made a major blunder in the mid-1950's when it launched a program to build more roads and mass-use facilities in the national parks. This unwise decision more than doubled the auto traffic inside the parks, produced "wilderness slums" where mass, mechanized camping was encouraged, and quickened the invasion of boats, mobile-campers and other machines.

George Hartzog, the current director of the park service, recognized that these lands are first and last nature parks, and that future public policies must be compatible with the highest concepts of conservation. But to disengage Americans from the "comforts" of their autos, to persuade them to walk or hike or climb into the solitary sections of the parks is no easy task. If the park service could start all over again, it is likely that most automobiles would be limited to the fringe areas, and quiet, low-polluting electric buses or "people movers" would be used to transport park visitors to overlooks or selected scenic areas. However, the auto already has a preferred place in the parks, and this solution will not be easy to accomplish.

There are, of course, other alternative solutions — but most of them are painful and some will require drastic changes in long-established policies.

Here are some solutions which can help the parks fulfill their highest functions:

1. Expand the Park System Itself

This was the main effort of the 1960's. Nearly ten new national seashores — from Cape Cod (Massachusetts) to Padre Island (Texas) to Point Reyes (California) — were acquired, and several new inland parks (most notably a section of California's unique redwood groves) were added. These new acquisitions helped, but their gains were more than offset by simultaneous population increases and greater mobility of the population.

2. Transfer Most Auto-Connected Camping to Areas Outside the Parks

This effort, too, is already underway. In the long run, it will mean encouraging the establishment of privately owned facilities of all kinds in nearby areas, and the development of more heavy-camping areas on adjacent national forests and other publicly owned lands.

3. Reorganize the Federal Government to Put the Land Management Function in a Single Department

President Nixon has proposed the creation of a new Department of Natural Resources to accomplish this. It deserves wide support, and would hasten the achievement of the goals outlined above.

4. Restore the Park Service to Its Nature Mission

This would minimize the impact of machine-oriented recreation in the parks. In a return to first principles, it would also recognize that the national parks are preeminently for people propelled by shank's mare — individuals who want to experience untrammeled nature for an hour, a day or a week. After all, our parklands constitute only a fraction of the total public estate: we should treat them as true nature preserves intended primarily for those who want intimate experiences with primitive America and the natural world.

5. Ration Access to the Overused Portions of Parks

This vital tool of park management is already being used. Wilderness uses are being controlled. The famous float trips through the Grand Canyon are soon to be rationed. And more "Full Up For Now" signs will appear in the congested areas of most parks. Rationing is an unhappy development, to be sure, but it is the only method we now have to protect the integrity of the parklands and give special meaning to the idea of "a national park experience." There is one sure way that determined people can avoid rationing. The spring and fall periods are the best time to see most of the parks. "Go in the off-season" is golden advice for those who want to study the parks in an atmosphere of quiet, solitary splendor!

As noted earlier, the U. S. national park concept has already inspired emulation in all parts of the world. In countries as diverse and far-flung as Japan, Kenya, Finland, Australia and Iran, scenic landscapes have been reserved and are being administered according

Heavy fog shrouds mossy mountain hemlocks in the North Cascades of Washington. New North Cascades National Park protects much of this mountain scenery.

Early visitors to the Wawona Big Tree in Sequoia National Park (left). Stephen T. Mather (right), first director of the National Park Service.

to the conservation concepts developed in this country. The belief that a nation has a moral duty to conserve its wonderlands for posterity has taken hold in many countries. Indeed, the Yellowstone lesson is now written large in the world.

In the long run (and park planning is meaningless unless it adopts the long haul perspective), there is reason to fear that the parks will succumb slowly to the pressures of growth — unless restraint becomes a new national imperative. If our demand for raw materials and other natural resources doubles four or five times by the year 2072, I believe it is certain that events will force us to exploit the petroleum and mineral deposits beneath our national parks. If the current statistical projections are fulfilled and the nation's population reaches, say, five hundred million in the next one hundred years, it is unlikely that the parks as we know them today can survive except as trampled remnants of the original America.

The late Joseph Wood Krutch, who fled New York twenty years ago and became one of the country's finest nature writers, foresaw this dilemma when he wrote:

> There are always rival claims to every unexploited area, and even the parks cannot stand up against such claims unless their own claim is recognized. Unless we think of intangible values as no less important than material resources, unless we are willing to say that man's need of and right to what the parks and wilderness provide are as fundamental as any of his material needs, they are lost . . . .

The generation now living may very well be that which will make the irrevocable decision whether or not America will continue to be for centuries to come the one great nation which had the foresight to preserve an important part of its heritage. If we do not preserve it, then we shall have diminished by just that much the unique privilege of being an American.

This is the big challenge as we quietly celebrate the Yellowstone centenary.

— Stewart L. Udall
Washington, D. C.

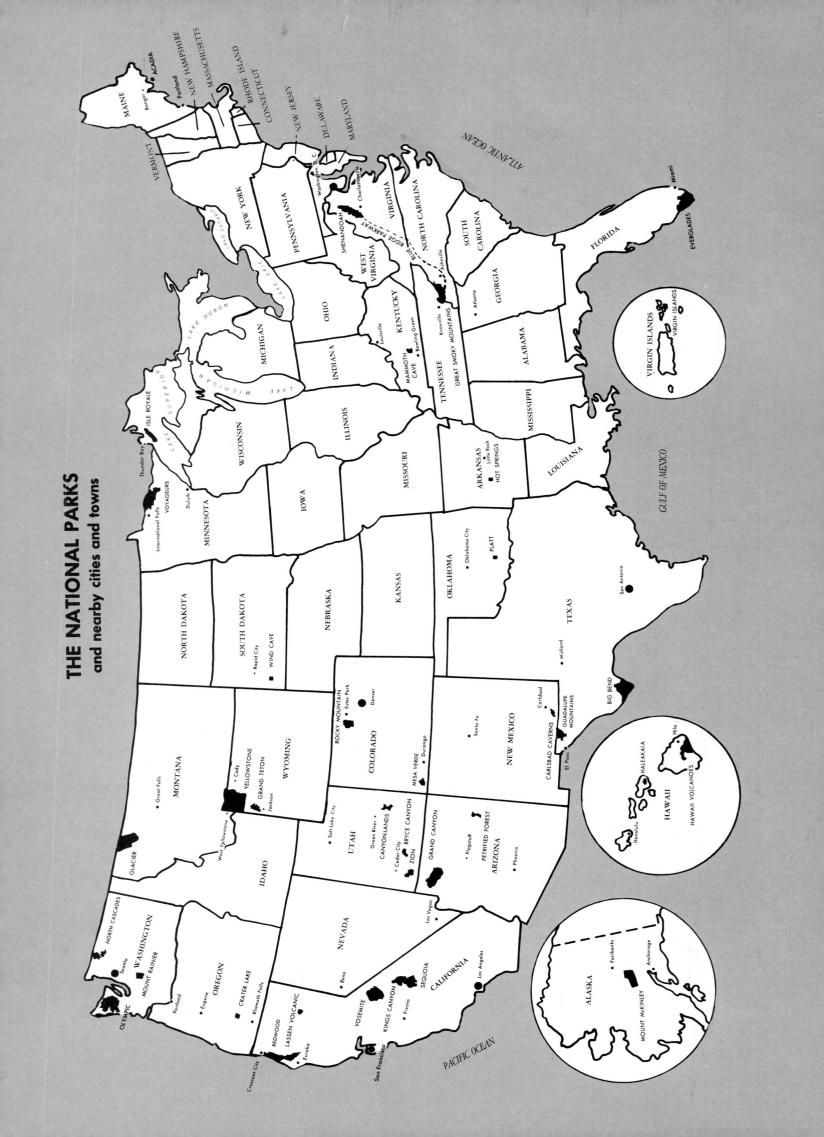

THE NATIONAL PARKS
and nearby cities and towns

ACADIA

LOCATION: Maine
(primarily Mount Desert Island)
SIZE: 41,642 acres
ESTABLISHED: 1919

There is an air of aristocracy about Acadia National Park, but nothing of the luke-warm, weak-tea flavor that sometimes surrounds that word. It is an "aristocrat" in the same sense that the noble Americans who first tried to preserve this place were called by that name — because they could appreciate the many moods of dashing splendor in man and nature.

Acadia National Park holds itself sometimes aloof in fog-shrouded mystery and sometimes spreads its inner resources of sea and sunshine with a lavish freedom born of ancient riches. Sometimes it flaunts its elegance unconcerned and unquestioning, and sometimes, with an overplus of hospitality, it opens its arms to any who come to its door.

It was here, after the Civil War, that the first families of America's inherited wealth came and invited the leisure classes of the world to join them for their summer pleasures. Like called to like, and those of princely tastes came to these islands of royal beauty.

Here is the pink granite of Cadillac Mountain (highest point on the Eastern Seaboard); here is the wild crashing sea surging into Thunder Hole; here are the wide, still waters of Somes Sound; here is the variety and grandeur of nature that brought the wealthy socialites of a by-gone age to vacation at Bar Harbor at the turn of this century.

This society has passed away. The Bar Harbor "cottager" whose "cottage" required a dozen household servants to maintain is no longer the chief visitor to Acadia, now, since 1919, a national park (called Lafayette National Park until 1929). The new aristocrat, the American vacationer appreciative of nature's wonders, comes bringing his family to this graceful leisure land where the smell of the great spruce forests and the briny tang of the sea, and the tangle of blueberries there for the picking, and the fish-filled streams for his rod and reel, and the lobster traps that are emptied at morning for his purchasing, these all let a man live like a king.

The name "Acadia" was first used in ancient Greece (in the form of "Arcadia") to mean a place of rest and delight-in-nature. Early French colonists found the name appropriate for the lands they settled in southeastern Canada, and when the area around Bar Harbor, Maine, became the first national park east of the Mississippi, it was appropriate that eventually it would be called Acadia National Park.

Most of the park is on Mount Desert Island which was discovered by Champlain in 1604. He named it "L'Isle de Monts-deserts," that is, "The Island of the Solitary Mountains." Jesuit missionaries settled there in the early 17th century to teach the Abnaki Indians who gathered there in the summer to harvest berries and to fish.

Plunging 107 feet into the Atlantic Ocean are the Otter Cliffs where the struggle between land and sea continues. Gulls and other birds dive for fish here and hoards of migrating sea ducks float by each season.

Other European settlers, French and English, followed. There were frequent clashes between these groups, but by 1759 France had relinquished its claim to the area, and New Englanders had established a settlement on Somes Sound (the only fjord on the New England Coast).

In 1820 Maine became a state and what is now Acadia National Park supported a thinly settled fishing economy. But during the 19th century artists rediscovered the beauty of the area, and summer boats from Boston brought it out of the wilderness and within the reach of the affluent, who responded to its loveliness. They came, summer after summer, building fashionable homes and fashioning an elegant summer society around themselves.

In 1901 some of those vacationers, fearful that the beauty of their island would be ravaged by commercial exploitation, formed a corporation "to acquire and hold for public use lands in Hancock County, Maine, [because of their] beauty [and] historical interest. . . ." They donated a square rod of land "for public use" [that is about 16 feet square: room enough perhaps for a bench and a drinking fountain), and in a dozen years had acquired about 6,000 additional acres. The corporation donated this land to the Federal Government, which, in 1916,

created out of this gift the 50 square miles that now make up Acadia National Park.

East of Mount Desert Island, across Frenchman Bay, there is another portion of the park on Schoodic Peninsula, and southwest of Mount Desert is the park's truly isolated wilderness of Isle au Haut ("High Island") which can be reached only by boat.

But to most of the visitors, who arrive in great numbers only to be swallowed by the winding trails and sheltered glens and surf-tossed beaches, Acadia National Park lies along the loop of Ocean Drive—a major park road curving along the Atlantic, gliding in and out of spruce and fir forests, dipping beside quiet inland ponds, suddenly surprising a feeding band of deer that with unfrightened speed gracefully vault into the deeper forest on one side of the road, with the elegance of the yachts, large and small, seen in the distance on the road's other side, sailboats spreading their chalk-white sails along the deep blue sea around them.

Most visitors come to Acadia in the summer, but spring and fall are pleasant too and the park is more one's own. Cool nights and rain are known to all three seasons. It is only winter — from December through April when snow and ice close the park road system — that is inhospitable.

*S*choodic Point (above) is at the tip of Schoodic *Peninsula, the only part of Acadia National Park located on the mainland. There, a young boy (left) feeds near-tame sea gulls on the rocks. Acadia's rockbound coast (far left) has come from centuries of ocean wear. On these shorelines, children can find a myriad of treasures mixed in with the ocean-smoothed rock; enough sea shells for a collection.*

The common egret (above left) was almost exterminated by plume hunters but now is Federally protected. Boaters (above right) still come to Bar Harbor. A sunset enhances Acadia's solitary feeling (below).

Acadia's miles of cliffs and rocky shorelines are easily accessible by scenic roads. Trails for hiking and for horses reach almost every spot in the park, varying from easy paths to rugged mountain routes.

BIG BEND

LOCATION: Southwestern Texas
SIZE: 708,221 acres
ESTABLISHED: 1944

The Great River, the Rio Grande, running a fairly straight southeast course, edging the United States and Mexico across the Chihuahua desert, suddenly bends around to its left, cuts to the north past the Chisos Mountains—for a total of 107 miles. And before it turns south again it puts a heart-shaped lower boundary on Big Bend National Park.

Here is the wilderness. Here is the unexplored. Here is the West (with a capital letter) in all of its desert and mountain and storybook wildness.

In this day of overcrowding bustle and hustle and nudging neighbors, parts of Big Bend National Park, which is within 300 miles of El Paso, Texas, and 400 miles of San Antonio, are still not fully explored. Parts of it are so untouched by this world of the 20th century that a vacationer can ride his horse out from the comforts of a modern resort area and within an hour feel that he is alone in a world, uninhabited, untouched, and perhaps—before he himself looked upon it—unseen.

This is a proud solitary stretch of country, harsh without bitterness, austere without anger and silent with a proud and brooding unfathomable mystery.

Even the suddenly green pockets of lush cotton-wood-lined oases along the river's edge seem like gentle guests (rather than settlers) of the sweeping mesa and rolling mountain land that tolerate their being there with the preoccupied hospitality of a host who has great matters on his mind.

This area has never been an easy one to know. It grudgingly permitted some acquaintanceship, but never sought or welcomed friendship; and it never offered itself or its resources to explorers or ranchers or miners or farmers. It wasn't until 1899 that anyone made a trip of record around the "big bend" of the Rio Grande. Others may have gone there before Robert T. Hill and five companions explored it for the Geological Survey in 1850, but the others went to raid, to smuggle or to hide.

Men who went there before the days of the park's development went there usually driven by motives which seemed better concealed than advertised. Train robbers, bank robbers, American fugitives, Mexican bandits slipped in and out of the area as they slipped in and out of the history of the outlaw-gunman West. Here, as late as 1916, Mexican bandits, possibly some of Pancho Villa's men, invaded the United States.

But today the men of violence are gone. Today if

The century plant stands before the Chisos Mountains in Green Gulch. The Chisos add a sense of adventure to their mysterious past: it was here that dinosaurs roamed before lava pushed upward to become mountains.

the visitor hears rustling in the underbrush, it is probably not a cattle rustler but a juvelina or a mule deer, or a cougar or a white tailed deer.

In the middle of the park, the Chisos Mountains rise up like a string of fortified castles set to hold back the advance of the hordes of sage and cactus on the desert floor. The mountains throw their forest troops into battle lines against the invaders. In the front rank are the stunted oak and drooping juniper, and on the higher ground, the piñon pine and Douglas fir and ponderosa pine.

The name of these mountains, "Chisos," is hard to translate. Part Indian, part Spanish, it carries the idea of ghostly wonder or enchantment in and out of both languages. And these mountains speak the mystery that surrounds Big Bend National Park.

Looking south from their south rim, a visitor knows in his mind that he is looking towards Mexico, but in the clear bright air and the isolated silence of a seemingly never-ending distance his heart begins to feel that he is looking over the edge of the world itself. He feels for just a moment on the edge of time itself so that, as a local saying has it, standing here on the side of the mountains of mystery, "on a clear day, you can see clear into the day after tomorrow."

Flowers begin to bloom in the lowlands in late February but do not reach the mountain heights until May. Spring also brings occasional "northers," sudden storms that bring chill winds and often dust. The mountains are particularly attractive in the summer when temperatures in the desert and valley hover around 100 degrees. With the end of autumn—warm, gentle and delicately colored—comes the sparkling clear air of winter. Once or twice a year snow comes to the mountains, but usually in winter the heights are merely brisk while the canyons remain comfortably warm during the day.

The river and mountains have given the park

three large canyons. Boquillas—or "Little Mouth"—
is where the river cuts the Sierra del Carmen in two.
In some places it cuts with the stroke of a butcher's
cleaver that slices the rock straight down to the
water's edge, and in other places it hacks with hatchet
chops that send chips of sand and tangles of willow
a few feet up the bank.

But up river in the Santa Elena Canyon the Rio
cuts the walls of the Grand Puerta ("Great Door")
with a 1,500-foot slash of its knife edge.

The third canyon, Mariscal ("Marshall"), is
most remote, most difficult to reach, and most rewarding. Mariscal allows only boatmen to explore its
limestone walls and view the fossilized remains of
animals who lived in those distant ages of the deep
past of our earth—times that still seem close beside
the traveler within the remote and mystic silence and
emptiness and untouched grandeur that is Big Bend
National Park.

*Santa Elena Canyon (above) continues for 17 miles
while sheer rock walls form a box-like gorge around
it. Here, the Rio Grande is an international border,
with Mexico on the left. Further along the river is
Boquillas, Mexico, (far left) an old village seated
below the Sierra del Carmen. In the northern section
of Big Bend is Dagger Flat, where the giant dagger
yucca (left) is found. Big Bend is the only place in
the United States where the giant dagger has grown.*

Queen Victoria (above) stands in the Queen's Garden below Sunrise Point. Variations in the weather and erosion resistance of the rock layers account for the unusually interesting forms at Bryce Canyon. Systems of cracks and joints have created such phenomena as the Natural Bridge (right) which was cut from the famous Pink Cliffs. The varying intensities of red are the result of the iron content of the rock.

BRYCE CANYON

LOCATION: Southern Utah
SIZE: 36,010 acres
ESTABLISHED: 1928

To enter Bryce Canyon is to come upon a unique world set in the middle of an already spectacular country. Its pinnacles and spires, in their strange, almost Gothic delicacy, create an impression that they are related to rock as lace is to fabric. The canyon is weird and other-worldly and at the same time inescapably an elemental, sculptural part of Earth. There *is* creation in destruction, and Utah's Bryce Canyon National Park is a silent, slowly evolving example of the forces of water seeking lower levels.

Stretching for about 30 miles along the eastern edge of 8,000-foot Paunsaugunt Plateau are the famous Pink Cliffs, one of the finest of Utah's eroded landscapes. Primordial forms (sometimes called "castles" and "temples"), have been constructed by the relentless forces of water rushing down the slopes of the plateau.

From atop the plateau rim, one looks out over the Bryce Amphitheatre and the Silent City, or into the narrows of the canyon called Wall Street, or over the vast expanse of land to the east and southeast where the Paria River for millenniums has capriciously cut, gouged and torn away layer upon layer of rock. The river and some relatively pencil-thin streams are now nibbling away at the rate of two feet every century.

The plateau is the edge of a bowl of color — oranges, reds, whites, pinks, yellows and purples interspersed with gentle browns, reflecting the changing light, from sunrise to sunset, from storm to sunshine, from summer to winter. Hardy visitors get a different and exciting glimpse of one of the superlatives of nature's handiwork, while hiking below the rim among the eerie but beautiful erosion remnants of the Wasatch-limestone formations.

Bryce Canyon's history began long before the Paiute Indians gave Paunsautgunt ("home of the beaver") Plateau its name and called the area, "red rocks standing like men in a bowl-shaped canyon." It was 60 million years ago that inland lakes and seas started to lay down on this area deposits of silt, sand and lime in beds as much as 2,000-feet thick. The deposition of the Bryce strata ended about 25 million years ago and the lands of southern Utah began to rise slowly. During this gradual elevation, produced by pressure within the earth, beds of rock were broken into blocks many miles in width and length. Some blocks were raised more than others, producing seven plateaus.

One of the area's early settlers was Ebenezer Bryce for whom the park is named. He pastured cattle here in the late 1870's and made the famous remark that it was "a hell of a place to find a stray cow." But it wasn't until the early 20th century that the remote canyon began to gain recognition as a potential park.

Today the park is everywhere enhanced by the trees, shrubs and flowers that nature has so expertly placed. Stately ponderosa pines, very old weather-beaten bristlecone pines, spruce, fir and junipers all abound. These in turn give a setting for the colorful birds, deer, fox and many other forms of wildlife. Bryce is geologically the youngest of the trio of truly great Southwest canyons, as unique in its own way as its older brothers, Grand and Zion.

A vivid contrast to the Pink Cliffs (above) is the three-foot snow that covers the area several months each year. Standing rigidly above the spires of Campbell Canyon is Boat Mesa (right) which rises over 8,000 feet.

CANYONLANDS

LOCATION: Southeastern Utah
SIZE: 337,258 acres
ESTABLISHED: 1964

This is a land where rock is master. It is everywhere in every form and shape imaginable, as if other objects had somehow been changed into it. You can see the sheer, vertical walls of a building, the swirls of a giant vat of rippled ice cream, the spires of a grand European cathedral, a Roman viaduct's arches, a waterfall's cascades, the pyramids of Egypt, the towers and columns of a Spanish castle—all are rock. The names of these fantastic rocks are as imaginative as the shapes themselves—Washerwoman Arch, Six-Shooter Peak, Silver Stairs, Spanish Bottom, Candlestick Spire, Dead Horse Point, Peekaboo Arch, Paul Bunyan's Potty.

Harsh yet delicate, this weather-streaked, time-worn rock country has a strange aura of mystery about it. Natural forces, the erosion of wind and water and the expansion of minute slivers of ice, sculptured these forms—this much we know. Desolate as they are, the "Canyon Lands," as they were called a few years ago, have such a fascination that visitors keep returning.

The center of Canyonlands is where the Green and the Colorado Rivers come together. And all around the confluence of these streams, the land is laced with tangles of small gorges down which, after a sudden cloudburst, a raging torrent will smash its violent way for an hour and then leave a dry and soon-dusty creek bed for perhaps another year, or even longer. Since the beginning of time this cut and slash of water has eaten away the land into a complex mass of sand and sagebrush and sandstone that is unmatched for variety. The heavier and constant flow of the main rivers, the Green and the Col-orado, have scooped out three large intersecting areas, between which it is difficult to move.

Some people have been lucky enough to sight-see Canyonlands from a helicopter. Light, low-flying airplanes have given others a sweeping panoramic glance at all of its treasures. With daring, experienced skill, and special boats it is possible to run through the now lazy, now rasping, tumbling, terrible waters of Cataract Canyon. Other waters can be traveled by rubber rafts, pontoons or motor boats. But for most of the park's modern vacation-explorers transportation is a tough, well-sprung car. And then there are some places one can only reach by walking, and yet still others to which you have to climb.

Coming in from the north, between the Green and Colorado rivers, the visitor moves along the skyline plateau to Grandview Point, on the southern tip of Island in the Sky, from which a great sweep of the park's high desert wilderness may be seen. Looking back to the north and west one can see the red round lift of Upheaval Dome which seems to bubble out of the earth's crust; and looking forward below him, the esplanade of White Rim, in a southern semicircle, puts a catwalk around the inner gorges. From there one looks down into a smaller arroyos, embayments and basins of lesser canyons.

West of the meeting of the rivers is the Land of Standing Rocks and a network of little-known, interlocking gullies and buttes called The Maze. Most of this area is broad upland plateau made up of vast, wild, overlaying, twisted and broken layers of rock — worn away by wind and occasional rain into shapes

The view south from Grandview Point shows variety in the canyons from mesas to spires, cliffs to plateaus.

that would seem to be the work of a madman.

The southeast section of the park, known as The Needles, is perhaps its most exciting part. Here the sandstone has been broken and eroded and pushed about into a jumble of pillars thrust-up, arches thrown-out and valley stamped-down into shapes so unusual that the visitor must learn new words to describe them.

The Grabens (from the German word for "ditch") are places where the land seems to have dropped down an elevator shaft, leaving behind them immense flat-bottomed valleys of stone bordered by vertical walls. And as the visitor comes upon these Grabens in this section of the park, such is the immensity of the surrounding distance, that what are deep faults in the earth's crust seem much smaller than they are.

Famous Druid Arch is also in this southeastern section of the park. Squarer than other natural-span formations, this arch looks like three balanced druid stones taken from England's mysterious Stonehenge on the Salisbury Plain — except that these rocks have

been multimagnified many times: instead of the menhirs being twice as high as a man can reach, these are about 220 feet high.

In this part of Canyonlands long departed Indians, or their predecessors, have left their mark. Storehouses of grain, with the corn still in them and dried iron-hard by a thousand summers, are still standing almost as they were left. Palm prints of prehistoric man are still visible on the walls of some caves. And at Newspaper Rock (outside Canyonlands' boundaries, at Utah's Indian Creek State Park, on the approach road to The Needles) the visitor can read the pictographs that someone scratched there on the "desert varnish" of the cliff. Here are man and animals, houses and hunters, circles and snakes, and symbolic rivers that must have meant something once to those who could read what was written here. But now these simple scratches on the canyon wall add to the wonderful solitude of Canyonlands' great empty space, another mysterious dimension of silence in the dim, forgotten past.

*A*ngel Arch (opposite) has an opening 190 feet high and was named for the figure of an angel with bowed head and folded wings leaning on his "harp." Druid Arch (left), like Angel Arch, is just south of The Needles area and resembles England's Stonehenge. Sandstone, broken into blocks by close-set joints, often is eroded to form such pillars, spires and balanced rocks. But strangely, the sandstone nearby was eroded into sunken valleys and swirls (below).

*I*n some cases, the approaches to a national park are as interesting as the park itself. Dead Horse Point (below), just north of the park, provides a mighty view of the Colorado River winding among the multihued and eroded rock faces as it heads into Canyonlands. From the same location (opposite, top), the varied, rugged nature of Canyonlands is starkly apparent. A jeep road makes its way between the cliffs only through the efforts of husky, energetic men (opposite, bottom) who have developed it.

CARLSBAD CAVERNS

LOCATION: Southeastern New Mexico
SIZE: 46,753 acres
ESTABLISHED: 1930

Plunging to a known depth of 1,100 feet are the Carlsbad Caverns, hollowed by seeping groundwater in limestone beds laid down by an ancient sea. Appropriately named, the Big Room (above) has 14 acres of floor space; at one point the ceiling arches 285 feet above the mile-long perimeter trail. Formations (left) include stalactites on the ceiling, stalagmites on the floor, columns and twisting helictites.

If one person can be credited with initially exploring the yawning depths of Carlsbad Caverns, in the contemporary record of man, it is a determined, brave and dedicated cowboy named James Larkin White, who descended into these incredible hollows in 1901.

Prior to his descent, this now world-famous national park of southeastern New Mexico had been known to a handful of ranchers, when the austere desert lands of the Guadalupe Mountains were settled just after the Civil War. But like most of our great natural wonders, the existence of the caverns was known to the Indians of the region and their forebears for many centuries prior to the incursions of the white man.

Cooking pits, colored clay paintings or pictographs attest to historic and prehistoric habitation in the sheltering vaulted arch of the caverns entrance.

For many years the awesome depths were known simply as the Bat Cave, from which hordes of the insect-eating mammals came wheeling and fluttering each summer day at sunset.

White so graphically described the bizarre features of this underground wonderland that the official interest of the General Land Office was aroused in 1923, and Robert A. Holley was assigned to investigate the authenticity of this vast natural wonder as an area possibly worthy of national preservation.

After 30 days of exploration, Holley was moved to state: "I am wholly conscious of the feebleness of my efforts to convey in words the deep, conflicting emotions, the feelings of fear and awe, and the desire for an inspired understanding of the Divine Creator's work which presents to the human eye such a complex aggregate of natural wonders in such a limited space."

On the basis of Robert Holley's enthusiastic official report, bolstered by the indefatigable efforts of James Larkin White, Carlsbad Cave was established as a national monument in 1923 and reestablished as a national park in 1930. Since then, about 13 million visitors have experienced the profound awe of both White and Holley. The breathtaking height of ceiling, the vastness of many-acred floor areas, the variety of exquisite forms to be seen on cavern roofs, walls and floors present proof that this is one of our na-

tion's most interesting and popular preservations.

On the surface of the park, especially in spring, there is a variety of colorful and bustling desert life. Birds, reptiles, raccoons, lizards and vultures thrive in the mountain-desert aridity which is emblazoned with the bright yellows of the bladderpod and prickly pear blossoms and blended with purple verbena and whitish pepperweed. Daytime temperatures in summer can be high, but evenings are cool. As summer wanes, the hillsides lose their color and reptiles go into hibernation beneath rocks. In winter the temperatures are mild, snow and ice are rare. Juncos, towhee and pyrrhuloxias become the most conspicuous of the birds.

And the bats still arrive en masse in spring, their return heralding the nightly tumbling black clouds of foraging flight emerging from the maw of the caverns. There is a proliferation of young bats each summer, but the chill frosts of November kill the insect provender, and mass migration southward again throws up a weird and sinuous cloud against exotic desert horizons.

Temple of the Sun (opposite) stands in the Big Room. At sunset from May to October, thousands of bats (above left) spiral from the entrance in search of food. Totem Pole (above right) is a huge, 40-foot stalagmite.

Wizard Island (above), situated in Crater Lake, is actually a volcano within a volcano. The caldera holding Crater Lake was formed when the volcanic cone of Mount Mazama collapsed. Visitors can take boat trips on this deep blue lake and even climb into the 90-foot-deep crater of Wizard Island. A 35-mile drive around the rim shows the size and scenic grandeur of the lake. Heavy snows from the moisture-filled clouds from the Pacific Ocean result in 50 feet of snow annually which lace the trees and shrubs (right) and ‘delight photographers. Despite such heavy snowfalls, the park stays open all year.

CRATER
LAKE

LOCATION: Southwest-Central Oregon
SIZE: 160,290 acres
ESTABLISHED: 1902

A quarrel between two mighty Indian gods created Oregon's Crater Lake — so goes the lore of the local prehistoric Indians who tell us that the earth collapsed to a depth of almost 2,000 feet, forming the circular lake's basin, because of a raging struggle between "chief of the world above" and "chief of the world below."

The myth, not quite as old as the actual geological earth movement of 7,000 years ago, which carved out the second deepest lake in the Western Hemisphere, tells us that the underworld deity retreated below just as the chief of the upper regions let fall a mountain top on any possible exit to the surface.

Yet science more factually hypothesizes that predecessors of the Indian myth-makers may have seen the collapse of volcanic Mount Mazama, thousands of years ago, and built their myth, like most myths, on a residue of fact.

Crater Lake, astride the Cascade Range, thence gathered to itself the snows and rains of centuries, tinged gradually into the vast and stunning royal blue of its present setting.

It is said that the lake has only two seasons: an eight-month, snow-shrouded winter and an Eden-like two-month summer. But there is a brief snow-melting spring, and a haunting, chill-touched momentary fall. Yet, in all seasons, there endures the onslaught of arboreal beauty with hemlock, fir and pine clothing the pumiced slopes in varied shades of green, dappling the warm tones of summer and richly dotting winter's wide, white mantle.

Mount Scott, highest point in the park at 8,926 feet,

commands the eastern side of the lake and overlooks blue waters 20 square miles in area. Multicolored canyon-like walls, 500 to 2,000 feet high, surround the crater depths of water, their heights majestic with conifers and bleak with sporadic barren surfaces.

The Pinnacles, near the eastern boundary, also contribute to the mute but striking evidence of earth forces that here wrought violence in the Olympian shaping of the now serene landscape.

John Wesley Hillman recalled, many years later, his initial encounter with Crater Lake on June 12, 1853. Only 21, he was perhaps the first white man to look upon Deep Blue Lake, as his party of exploration chose to call it. His recollection: "It is really an impossibility to describe this lake as I first viewed it. The vast loneliness of the place, the sparkling water so many feet below, the beautiful view of the whole thing are all too great to be described; one must see them to appreciate them."

Others followed Hillman, but not until 1869 did visitors from Jacksonville give the vast volcanic repository of handsome waters its present name.

William Gladstone Steel is outstanding among the lake's subsequent admirers. He came, for the first of many visits, to the brink on August 15, 1885. A six-day sojourn lengthened into a lifetime rendezvous. On one trip, in 1888, Steel was inspired to comment: "Standing alone, like a sentinel on the mountains of the Far West, [Crater Lake] looks down on the sleeping grandeur about it and is unique in all the world. The day is coming when the people of all nations will gather to view its grandeur, then return to their homes to wonder that such things can be."

This indeed was a prophecy, aided and abetted by his own dedication and labors. Leader of the 17-year campaign to create a national park, he achieved this goal when, on May 22, 1902, President Theodore Roosevelt signed the bill conferring on the wondrous waters their present status. Will Steel, later superintendent and U.S. commissioner for the park, has since been informally and gratefully called: "Father of Crater Lake National Park."

Thus was the immortal blue of Crater Lake preserved for the beneficence of mortal man and his posterity.

A golden-mantled ground squirrel, often confused with a chipmunk, is very popular with park visitors.

The Phantom Ship (opposite), with 175-foot spires, "floats" before the lava cliffs that surround the second deepest lake in this hemisphere. The 8,926-foot Mount Scott (above) is the highest point at Crater Lake.

EVERGLADES

LOCATION: Southern Florida
SIZE: 1,400,533 acres
ESTABLISHED: 1947

Known for its birdlife and open spaces, Everglades was called "Pa-hay-okee" or "grassy waters" (above) by the Indians. The osprey (left), the only hawk that dives into water, sails toward his nest in a dead tree.

Quiet, calm, flat, mysterious — the Everglades are a unique part of the American landscape, the largest subtropical wilderness in North America.

The Calusa and Tequesta Indians first settled here, flourishing among the mangroves and thriving on the rich fish and game varieties in swamp and stream. Both groups dwelt in this sweeping, water-haunted lushness before the beginning of the Christian era. The Calusa, however, survived as an identifiable tribe for 250 years after the Spanish explorers arrived in the 16th century.

The legend of the fierce, quaintly bonneted, and riotously painted Seminole Indians, whom we more familiarly associate with the Everglades, goes back to the early 19th century when that tribe fled the plains before the U.S. Cavalry. Now, they fish in the park, amid nostalgic overtones.

Lake Okeechobee, massively spilling over to the north, created this river of grass, broad, short and shallow, with multifarious water creatures thriving in and about its swampy lushness, characterizing the biological wealth of the area.

Leggy, wading birds lift their fishy meals from the waters; alligators, turtles, otter and fish flutter, creep and splash in natural patterns through the willows, submerged roots, drenched grass and spatterdock.

All this lush, growing green can be seen best from the jungle spots on elevated islands which are called hammocks. Towering trees, dangling vines, carpets of ferns, West Indian in character, flourish here, where thrive the Liguus tree snails, so beautiful in aspect and so rarely seen elsewhere.

Here, where dark, tangled coastal forests drove Spanish horsemen to more maneuverable coasts, are ghostly clusters of mangrove trees, cypress heads, bay-heads and stands of Caribbean pine. Many trees grow above tangles of crooked roots which sustain their trunks above the water. The roots interlock and are a hazard to the legs of men landing from pole-propelled flatboats. The pines are slender-tufted, fire-resistant and fire-perpetuated and they have been used extensively in the building of termite and rot-resistant structures.

Hauntingly characteristic of the demesne is the whispering in the pinelands aroused by the slightest breeze, wafting a heady fragrance through the trails frequented by students of nature.

These tree concentrations are called "the mountains of the glades" rising with their own minute majesty only seven feet above sea level. Yet even in the wettest seasons they are not inundated. This is the plashy purlieu of the raccoon, the bobcat, quail and turkey.

The Everglades thermometers do not fluctuate sharply during the two characteristic seasons, the wet summer and dry winter. But the two contrasting seasons obviously influence the wildlife, with bird and beast migrating in winter to surviving water areas in great numbers.

During the rainy season, great cloud formations are sculptured battlements over the terrain, colored and dominated by dark thunderheads. The clouds progressively reach an explosive peak, then burst with a great rush, pouring down the life-giving rain. Sometimes a hurricane will move in from the tropical seas, wreaking havoc on trees, branches, birds and fish in mighty climax over the park. Sea beasts are washed ashore in the wake of the storm's anger; vegetation stands bare and wind-stripped; water everywhere, salt and fresh alike, inundates the land.

Midway to Flamingo from park headquarters, the salt area begins. This enormous brackish zone is nature's inaccessible nursery for numerous game fish and the coveted pink shrimp. Nature has providently arranged here a no-man's-land where predatory man and beast do not venture. Thus, spawn and prawn, a swampy matrix of infant, edible fish life, is permitted to grow and eventually fills the demands of

commercial and sport fish operations amid the Keys and along the Gulf Coast. This rich nursery of marine edibility actually is the basis of the well-known shrimp industry in the Tortugas.

Here, too, are the ghostly forests of mangrove trees, grotesque on the aforesaid prop roots, arching over sinuous waterways in hardy challenge to the boatman. The citizen of Copenhagen would wonder at the rookeries of storks in this region, increasing and multiplying, a continent removed from the storied stork-nest roofs of Denmark.

The dark memory of the ruthless plume hunters can be vividly recalled in this expanse, where ruthless exploiters once threatened to bring exquisite species

On Cape Sable the mangrove tree, which inhabits tidal marshes, stands on a maze of remarkable aerial roots.

of waterfowl to the point of extinction.

Flamingo, once a rustic, fishing village is now a gala gateway to the water wilderness of the park, the bays and rivers. Along the rich and intriguing Florida Bay shore there is no perceptible dividing line between land and sea. Beyond is Cape Sable, an arching shell beach, a pristine retreat whose immaculately white sands shelter the eggs of huge, lumbering loggerhead turtles, which may grow to weigh nearly half a ton.

The park by night is a jungle of sound and movement. The cries of night birds, the watery thrashings of alligators seeking garfish in the sloughs, the crackling predatory movements of raccoons and panthers, the choruses of insects, toads and frogs arise in sporadic crescendo, and all are weirdly, momentarily illuminated by streaks of lightning in the ebony sky.

The experienced explorer knows the threat and rudeness of the terrain. The danger in some places of poisonous snakes (including the deadly diamondback rattlesnake), and trees which shake off blister-yielding rain drippings, the pits and pinnacles of the trails, make some tourists wary. Add to this the steamy humidity of summer, the severe winds and drenching rains. But the prize is worth the worry and strain. It now is attainable in areas of minimal discomfort for the bird-watcher, the naturalist, the boater. The strange beauty of the Everglades is ours.

One of the Everglades famous wading birds, the American egret spends the dry season (winter) in its rookery.

His head rising just above the water, a bull alligator (opposite, upper left) inflates his throat for a mating call. Differing from a crocodile in jaw and teeth formation, the alligator's biggest enemy, after maturity, is man. A frog (opposite, upper right) makes an interesting pattern while sunning itself on a palm leaf. The cougar or puma (opposite, below) sloshes along a tidal channel. It is seldom seen for there are only 100-300 left on the entire eastern seaboard, all in Florida. Everglades National Park is a good refuge for wildlife because hunting is prohibited. A small road off Florida State Highway 29 passes tall stately royal palm trees (above) which are native to southern Florida.

*T*wo *Seminole children (above) stand before their huts deep in the swamps near U.S. Highway 41. After Gen. Andrew Jackson ended the Seminole War (1817-1818), most Seminoles fled west, but many escaped to live in the glades of southern Florida. Their houses are built above ground, for low spots fill during the rainy season of summer. The wood and leaves from the palm tree (right) are used for Seminole homes.*

*D*ead and rotting logs lay across a vast swamp (below) which is interlaced with placid waterways. At Everglades many tropical plants, as well as animals, are interspersed with plants and animals found in the temperate zone. This subtropical wilderness is the largest in North America. The cormorant (right), frequently seen in the Royal Palm Area, is an expert fisherman who often swims with just its neck and head showing and then dives sharply to pursue and capture a fish in its strongly hooked beak.

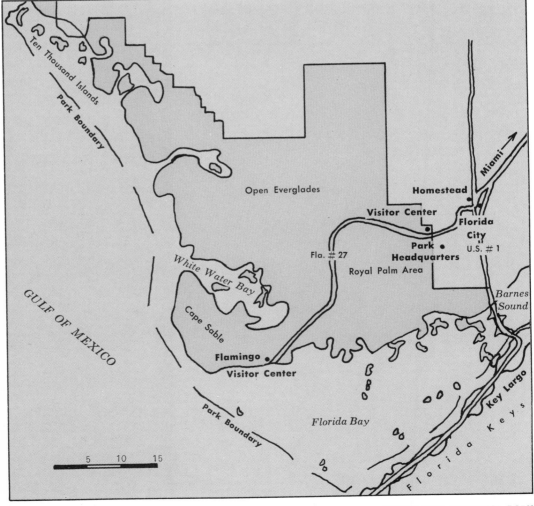

Ten Thousand Islands

Park Boundary

Open Everglades

Homestead

Miami

Visitor Center

Florida City

Fla. # 27

Park Headquarters

U.S. # 1

Royal Palm Area

White Water Bay

Barnes Sound

GULF OF MEXICO

Cape Sable

Flamingo

Visitor Center

Key Largo

Park Boundary

Florida Bay

Florida Keys

5   10   15

EVERGLADES NATIONAL PARK

GLACIER

LOCATION: Northwestern Montana
SIZE: 1,013,129 acres
ESTABLISHED: 1910

Under the brooding storm clouds a sunrise reflects on Little Chief Mountain to the left and Citadel Mountain in the rear on the shore of St. Mary Lake. In 1932, Canada and the United States expressed good will by combining adjacent Glacier National Park in the United States and Waterton Lakes National Park in Canada into Glacier-Waterton International Peace Park.

Upper St. Mary Lake is an icy, elongated sphere of blue — a sapphire of water worn like a jewel, mirroring wisps of cotton clouds and wearing the sharp lines of surrounding mountains as the hands upon the face of a clock. The massive peaks, sheer, sharp walls of stone, are the rulers of this empire of trees and water and wildlife, flower-strewn meadows and living glaciers existing almost side by side in paradoxical enjoyment of their environments.

Here there are the seekers of this extraordinary beauty, the "Crown of the Continent," which includes more than a thousand miles of trails which lace through nearly 1,600 square miles of wild loveliness.

The ice-fingers of earth-evolution are not far from the velvety grass spread of hills and valleys sprinkled with summer flowers, one of the four biological life zones found here. Above are the spruce and fir, and surmounting them are subalpine plants, while still farther lie the colors — green, white and pastels — which hint at life in the most improbable places. Snow-capped peaks touch the limits of the sky a mile or more above the looking glasses of over 200 lakes.

The joyous sound of rushing water fills the spectator's ears, the pounding of diamond-blue streams cascading over moss-strewn stones and the never-ending roar of waterfalls tossing dancing crystals into the air above, defying time to stop their existence.

The geological history of the land is the foundation upon which this extraordinary beauty rests; plants and animals, fish and fowl are here because of the chain of events which evolved to form this panorama, from its rugged peaks mantled with snow to the green spread of meadows and valleys.

The heights arrived when the Rockies came into being 60 million years ago, but while that great stretch of peaks rose, new forces vised this Canadian-border region, bringing it sharply together, forcing the infant mountains sideways until finally the folded earth broke under the strain. The pressure continued, edging the land to the east for almost 40 miles.

Sedimentary layers — silts, sands, clays and muds — started it all a billion or two years ago in the shallow arm of a prehistoric sea. Chemical changes coupled with time and pressure solidified the layers, and they submerged, then emerged.

A million years ago, the valley floors lay beneath great glaciers which relentlessly ground downhill. They gave way years ago to smaller masses of ice, but not before the park's valleys were filled with ice three-fifths of a mile high. Then the earth became warm again, and magically the ice disappeared, then returned in lesser fury to cover the earth once more.

There is still preponderous evidence of the glaciers here, despite the warming trend. Nearly 300 acres are still covered by Sperry Glacier, about 400 feet deep, a latter-day, and comparatively miniscule, sample of what helped shape this region. Those flowing rivers of ice of a million years ago grabbed particles of sand and massive boulders, edging them along to rasp at the landscape and form today's rugged spectacle.

The hewn earth is a natural habitat for 57 species of animals and 210 bird species, some of which rest a day or two twice a year during migration.

The Rocky Mountain goat uses its soft-centered, splayed hooves to grasp the precarious cliffs, along with the pika and marmot and an occasional wolverine. In the deep, green depths of the forests live moose, elk, whitetail and mule deer, and black and grizzly bears. Above them wheel hawks and eagles, their telescopic eyes seeking food, and grouse escape in a thunder of wings from underfoot. Thrushes sing anonymously from the thick undergrowth, while the slaty-gray dipper flits along swiftly flowing streams. Harmonizing with the cacophony of bird sounds is the angry shriek of the jays preaching from the pulpit of treetops over the steady tree-drumming of the scarlet-crested pileated woodpecker, pausing only to vent its feelings about insect-hunting expeditions deep beneath tree bark. Beneath the surface of rushing streams and the translucent mirror of lakes live 22 species of fish: trout, salmon, whitefish, grayling.

It is little wonder Indians found their way here and chose it as a place to live for about 10,000 years. The Kutenai were displaced by the Blackfeet more than 200 years ago, and it was possibly their hostility that kept the Lewis and Clark expedition from the region. The Blackfeet received $1.5 million for their lands in 1890 when a copper strike was announced, and thus the region became open to a new generation of explorers.

Their reservation, an attraction in itself, adjoins

In early summer, yellow glacier lilies dot Logan Pass with color below the Garden Wall, seen to the north.

the park to the east where some of them sometimes gather in the colorful garb and feathered headdresses of their ancestors.

But color is not confined to the dyed feathers, for here is an area south of the Canadian border where a subarctic climate exists, giving life in short but magnificent splendor to alpine flowers. Up and down the great expanses of land are glacier lilies, their yellow blossoms contrasting with the blue of gentians and the scarlet of monkey-flowers. The lower landscapes are dominated by the cone-bearing trees, sometimes dripping needles upon Lake McDonald, the largest of the bodies of water, nestled in the loving grasp of western red cedar, with its fernlike leaves, hemlock and yew. The most common tree in the park is the lodgepole pine, which occurs on both slopes of the park, growing in pure stands or mixed with spruce, fir and Douglas fir. The needle-losing "evergreen"

is the western larch. In autumn, its golden-yellow needles stand out in bright contrast against a background of forest greenery.

During the brief summer, sudden rain squalls or thundershowers may occur, and the higher elevations are cool at all times of the year. Even at the lower levels it is chilly after the sun sets.

The hasty traveler will see a part of this by driving across the park on the Going-to-the-Sun Road, the only road to cross the park. But this is only a hint of what lies beyond the long stretch of modern creation. A mountain never truly unfolds until one has stood at its feet or feasted upon the valleys below its peak; a green forest does not reveal its unique charms unless one stands under its pyramid spires; nor do nature's charms become fully apparent until one takes a few moments for silent appreciation. Glacier was meant to be felt, not idly viewed.

*B*eargrass (left), which is not a grass but a lily, blooms along the slope of 9,604-foot Going-to-the-Sun Mountain above Logan Pass Road. So common and showy is the beargrass that it is considered to be the park flower. With over 1,000 miles of trails, such as Skyline Trail (above), Glacier has the most extensive trail system of all the national parks.

Flowering until July, the Indian paintbrush (above left) decorates the Going-to-the-Sun Road. A close-up of the glacier lily (above right) which will grow on the edge of snow banks and sometimes up through the snow.

Flinsch Peak (opposite) is an excellent example of a cirque or amphitheatre caused by ice erosion. The pot-holes are also from glaciation. Pink monkey-flowers (below) bloom below the Garden Wall, a long cliff face.

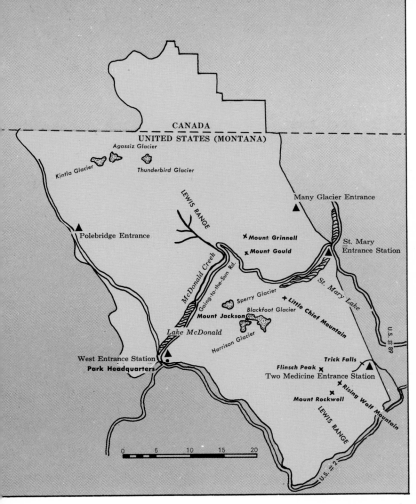

GLACIER NATIONAL PARK

*O*verlooking Two Medicine Valley (opposite, above) from abandoned lookout above Blackfeet Highway, one sees Rockwell Mountain in the center and Rising Wolf Mountain on the right. Light clouds cover 8,848-foot Mount Grinnell and Grinnell Glacier (opposite, below) on the eastern edge of the Continental Divide. Trick Falls (right), in the Two Medicine area, is named because, in summer, after the melted snows of spring have subsided, the relatively low water flow is through a hidden opening in the base.

GRAND CANYON

LOCATION: Northwestern Arizona
SIZE: 673,575 acres
ESTABLISHED: 1919

At the Grand Canyon's South Rim, one stands at the brink of grandeur, looking over the Colorado to the higher North Rim. After Theodore Roosevelt's visit in 1903, he described the canyon "as the one great sight every American should see."

Late sunlight illuminates the walls of Deva, Brahma and Zoroaster "temples" near the North Rim.

Of all the geographic features of the United States that are famed for their scenic grandeur, the most extraordinary, the most truly unique, is the mile-deep canyon which the Colorado River has carved across the high plateaus of northwestern Arizona. . . . Though there are elsewhere deep canyons, some of even greater depth than the Grand Canyon, . . . there is not one that can match its vastness, its majesty, its ornate sculpture and its wealth of color. Whoever stands upon the brink of the Grand Canyon beholds a spectacle unrivaled on this earth.

FRANCOIS E. MATTHES, *The Grand Canyon of the Colorado River*

The wind blows gently down this vast wound in the earth, rippling the surface of its creative force, the river, and carrying occasional small puffs of red dust from the awesome walls. The breeze wanes and the eerie silence fans out in four directions, held captive within the impenetrable fortress nature spent nine million years to create.

The Grand Canyon is true to its name, yet a mere, momentary glance prods the beholder's mind, searching for a word more expressive than "Grand." The majestic, water-wrought stone sculpture is 217 miles long, averages a mile deep and spreads nine miles across in a panorama of pastels, each a page in the book of the canyon's continuing evolution.

In places where the bottom can be reached, the long hike or ride on muleback gradually unfolds in a geological layer cake — gray limestone walls formed when a long-forgotten sea shimmered in the prehistoric sunlight; green shale holding primitive fossils; pastel layer upon pastel layer, until finally millions of years have been passed in a drop of three-fifths of a mile. In the Inner Gorge are sheer walls growing progressively darker as they plunge toward the rushing Colorado River, walls so ancient they were formed before life on the earth, their fossilless bulk existing in the dark centuries when creation was building its foundation.

The river is still building the Grand Canyon, widening it and deepening it an unmeasurable, infinitesimal fraction of an inch each year. Where a narrow suspension bridge hangs frailly across the Colorado, the pulsating red torrent which carried, until the closure of Glen Canyon Dam in 1963, a half-million tons of soil downstream each day, each abrasive bit gently, imperceptibly wearing away at the captive walls, loosening other particles in the interminable process of erosion. Today it carries approximately one-sixth as much sediment.

In 1869 its vastness lured John Wesley Powell, the great explorer, here to lead a long and daring expedition through the treacherous canyons and gorges. The Spanish conquistadores stood upon its edge in the mid-1500's, and American trappers visited it in the 18th century, but it remained for Powell to conquer the Colorado.

A topographer, Lt. Joseph Christmas Ives, viewed the canyon in 1858, and later wrote, "It seems intended by nature that the Colorado River, along the greater portion of its lonely and majestic way, shall be forever unvisited and undisturbed." A geologist with Ives, John S. Newberry, did not share Ives' gloomy thoughts, and later interested Powell in the expedition. To Powell, the dangerous trip was a labor of unbridled joy. "Past these towering monuments, past these mounded billows of orange sandstone, past these oak-set glens, past these fern-decked alcoves, past these mural curves, we glide hour after hour, stopping now and then as our attention is arrested by some new wonder," Powell wrote.

The splendor of the canyon has changed little

Shadows enhance the rugged forms of the canyon in the view from Point Imperial on the North Rim.

since the Powell expedition. There are still the sheer walls, tiny rills tinkling across the red stone and patches of green here and there, sprinkled in improbable places, defying gravity and the elements.

Hardy Indians wrested a livelihood from the forbidding land, but each day must have been a supreme effort. Evidence of primitive hunters 3,000 and more years old has been discovered in dry caves. Twigs were cut, split and twisted into semblances of animals, as if the ancients created them in hope they would materialize into living creatures for food.

The hunters sought more fertile lands, and in their place came the Basketmakers, followed by the Pueblo tribe and its intricate culture. They lived in the area for about 600 years and their villages are among the more than 500 Indian sites found within the confines of the 1,050-square-mile park.

Maidenhair fern and other green plants are fed by a little waterfall as it splashes down Elves' Chasm.

The Navajo and Hopi live on reservations to the east of the park while the dwindling Havasupai dwell in a small area in the western section of Grand Canyon. The 200 Havasupais, whose tribal name means "people of the blue-green water," farm a small valley irrigated by Havasu Creek.

This lush valley, with its docile, sequestered people, is in sharp contrast with much of the canyon where a forbidding desert spreads beneath the rims. The bighorn sheep has found survival difficult here, and its barren stretch has isolated on the Kaibab Plateau to the north a tiny colony of tufted-eared tree squirrels, the rare Kaibab.

South of Grand Canyon are the San Francisco Peaks, which reach 12,670 feet, the highest in Arizona. From their peaks to the depths of the canyon is a range of plant and animal life encompassing the identical varieties a traveler would find on a track from the Arctic Circle to northern Mexico, each having found its ecological niche in this relatively small section of a wild and free place.

The spectacle of the canyon from the air is indescribable; flat stretches of unbroken stone suddenly turning 90 degrees and dropping thousands of feet to the silvery knife of water appearing as a line of indolent mercury beneath the noon sun.

Within the canyon, the insignificance of man is realized with the first uplift of the eyes to rims above, dark shadows creasing the walls in the foreground and blue-hazed peaks beyond the next bend in the river. Here and there are wide places where the river's current has slowed a bit, depositing sand and silt on a narrow bank where a little green flourishes.

To those who find their greatest appreciation of the canyon from within it, rather than standing on the rims, and looking below, Theodore Roosevelt was moved to say when the century was only three years old: "In the Grand Canyon, Arizona has a natural wonder which, so far as I know, is in kind absolutely unparalleled. I want to ask you to do one thing in connection with it in your own interest and in the interest of the country — to keep this great wonder of nature as it now is. I hope you will not have a building of any kind . . . or anything else to mar the wonderful grandeur, the sublimity, the great loneliness and the beauty of the canyon. Leave it as it is. You cannot improve on it. The ages have been at work on it, and man can only mar it."

While snow falls on the rim (above), the temperature may be 50 degrees at the bottom of the canyon. Prickly pear blossoms (overleaf) bloom with the dark wall of the South Rim in the background.

*T*he Inner Gorge of the Colorado River (left) as the late afternoon sun illuminates red limestone formations. View through an arch on the South Rim (below), the rim most often frequented by park visitors. Arizona State Highway 67 (lower right) leads visitors to the North Rim. After a passing rain storm (right), dark clouds rise above the North Rim.

*N*ine million years ago the Colorado River began to cut through land while the land slowly rose and today the mile-deep Grand Canyon exposes two billion years of geologic history (left). Its width of nine miles came from landslides which provided abrasive material to deepen the channel further. After a summer rainstorm, a rainbow bends (opposite) into the canyon passing a ponderosa pine standing on the rim.

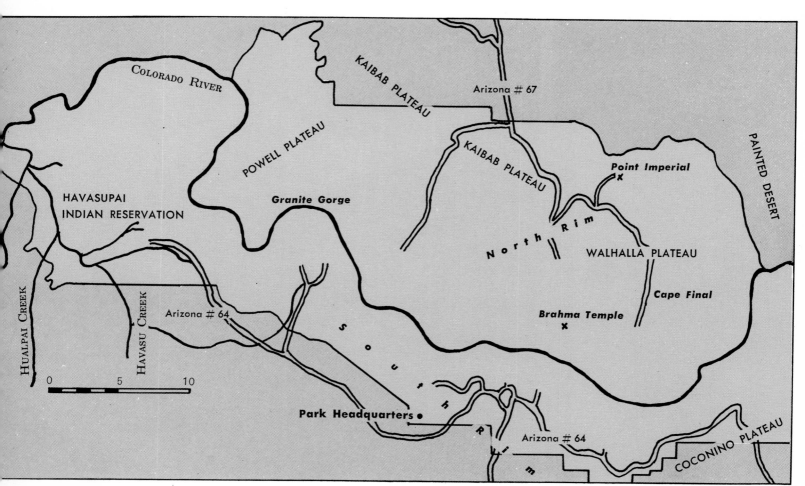

COLORADO RIVER

KAIBAB PLATEAU

Arizona # 67

KAIBAB PLATEAU

POWELL PLATEAU

Point Imperial
x

HAVASUPAI
INDIAN RESERVATION

Granite Gorge

N o r t h   R i m

PAINTED DESERT

WALHALLA PLATEAU

HUALPAI CREEK

HAVASU CREEK

Arizona # 64

Cape Final

Brahma Temple
x

S o u t h

0   5   10

Park Headquarters •

R i m

Arizona # 64

COCONINO PLATEAU

GRAND CANYON NATIONAL PARK

GRAND TETON

LOCATION: Northwestern Wyoming
SIZE: 310,350 acres
ESTABLISHED: 1929

Mount Moran, reflected in Buffalo Fork of the Snake River, is flat-topped because sediment covers jagged rock beneath. The Teton's incredible peaks have drawn Indians, trappers, cattle men and tourists to this exciting, rugged land.

Vast, snow-covered graph lines of gray are etched upon the spring-breath blue of sky, mirroring their mighty heights upon apparently miniscule lakes below; giant shadows are cast across already-dark forests of deep green.

The Tetons give no hint of their ascension; no telltale foothills lead the viewer's eyes gradually to this grandiose essence of all the beauty that the mountains of the West have to offer; for here there is a glassy lake, a stand of conifers and suddenly there are those incredible peaks.

Through the great valley pours the Snake River, a wide and rushing stream flowing clearly across a deep bed of sand and stones where gamefish dart in cool depths and to which adventurous man escapes

An old whitebark pine stands on a hillside below the Grand Teton in the center of the Cathedral Group.

for a few moments to ply the current in a fragile rubber raft.

Lakes lie among the green like a cool morning's dew on a field of newly mown grain, glistening in the sun between the natural fist of the Tetons on one side and wind-whispered forests of conifers on the other. Here and there are sun-splashed meadows, a crown of green wearing the royal jewels of complacent wildflowers and streams trickling through rich, black humus where the colors of spring blooms push their way through the floor of last autumn's fallen leaves. This forest is not silent, for there is the pleasure grunt of the moose with newfound food, the chattering of thousands of birds feeding and the scrape then crash of a long-dead tree as the black bear uncovers a delicacy of insects burrowed beneath. There is the hoof of the deer as a doe leads her fawn to shoots of green ready to burst through the carpet of the forest.

The graceful mule deer pick their way down mountain trails in fall, seeking vegetation in the valleys below. High above are a few bighorn sheep, laboring among the rocks finding forage, while thousands of American elk (wapiti) move through the park in herds. In autumn, the big-chested bull elks trumpet mightily, the sound echoing and re-echoing as they lead their harems through the forest.

There are some birds here in winter, but in summer more than 200 species from bee-sized hummingbirds to eagles and soaring falcons congregate. This peaceful place even attracts the rare trumpeter swan.

Each season unfolds something new; yellow masses of buttercups spring forth shortly after the snow melts, followed by violets, spring beauties, yellow fritillary, the mariposa lily and shooting stars. Calypso orchids hide their delicate beauty in damp and dark corners, while late-blooming gentians begin to unfold as summer's heat wanes. On the peaks, where the warmth lasts but a few weeks, alpine flowers bud, blossom and go to seed in a matter of days.

The mountains are hard, crystalline rock, hugging, in part, Cascade Canyon where a trail rims beaver-built ponds and crosses meadows, skirting great slashes of boulders on hillsides. The valley of Jackson Hole is filled with rock and gravel too porous to hold water, and is therefore covered with the tenacious sagebrush, common to semidesert regions.

The Tetons' beginning was nine million years

An all-day journey down the Snake River takes one past the Cathedral Group which stands over 13,000 feet above sea level. Later the river picks up speed going through narrow channels and small but exciting rapids.

ago when a chunk of earth was thrust up along the west side of Jackson Hole. The crack in the surface, Teton fault, divided the masses of rock. To the east, they sank, and to the west rose slowly. The high country formed the Tetons, then perhaps some 20,000 feet above sea level. Erosion worked upon the peaks, sending showers of rock and stone into the valley, then glaciers completed the task in the Ice Age as the sandpaper effect wore away sharp ridges, filling gorges, then water put the finishing touches on these great natural works.

The precipitous east face is what remains of the gigantic fault which began the process. Beneath it lies the valley, relatively flat and even, because of the sinking process. The lakes were holes created by glaciers, and the depressions scattered across the floor of Jackson Hole were formed when huge blocks of ice, the leavings of the glaciers, became buried. When they melted, their coverings collapsed.

The beginning of the 19th century saw the last of Indian control over the Grand Tetons. John Colter, a former member of the Lewis and Clark expedition, explored the area in 1807, the first of a line of hunters and trappers. Teton Pass was crossed by the Astorians in 1811 on their way to fortune in the Northwest. The French-Canadian trappers found their way here, naming the Grand, Middle and South

Teton mountains "Les Trois Tetons," or "The Three Breasts." The great and rugged mountain men, Jim Bridger, Jedediah Smith and David Jackson, for whom the Hole is named, lived and trapped here, reaping the bounty of valuable furs bestowed on the remote region. *The Virginian,* a classic Western novel by Owen Wister published in 1902, did much to publicize the area.

The trappers have vanished, along with the hunters, and in their footsteps walk a new breed of adventure-seekers, the mountain climbers. The Tetons are classed by experts as among the best in the world, since there is a mountain here to match every skill from steep footpaths to sheer walls of solid granite, affording pitons a safe and secure footing. The classic climb is 13,766-foot Grand Teton which takes about two days with an overnight camp about 11,500 feet up. Other recreational attractions include boating down the Snake River, fishing in the clear blue lakes and streams and hiking the miles of trails.

Grand Teton National Park was established in 1929, and in 1950 Congress added another 52 square miles to it, the gift of John D. Rockefeller, Jr. It brought the total to about 473 square miles, a spectacular corner of the United States where nature is the great equalizer, enthralling all who reap this majestic scene with their eyes.

The Teton Range is a gigantic block in the earth's crust uplifted along a 40-mile long fault, a zone of weakness, and then carved out by glacial action.

The Episcopal Chapel of the Transfiguration (above) at Moose Entrance Station is one of many religious centers at the national parks. Jackson Lake (overleaf) at the foot of the Tetons in the central section.

Climbers (left) work their way up Teton Glacier on Grand Teton Mountain. The two-day strenuous climb to the summit of "The Grand" can be made only with permission from the park's Mountaineering Headquarters and never alone. Jackson Lake (above) is popular with boaters, skiers and sailors. This wide lake in Jackson Hole was formed from the waters of melted glaciers after the relatively recent Ice Age.

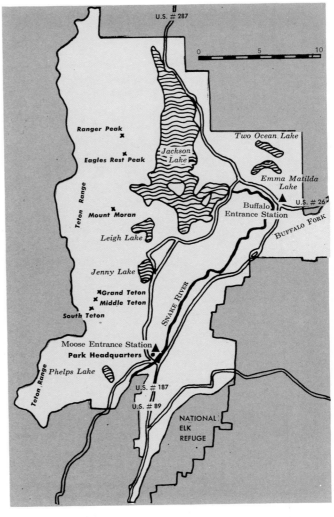

GRAND TETON NATIONAL PARK

85

GREAT SMOKY MOUNTAINS

LOCATION: Western North Carolina
and Eastern Tennessee
SIZE: 516,626 acres
ESTABLISHED: 1930

Rising high between the states of North Carolina and Tennessee are the Great Smoky Mountains, the highest range of the Appalachian Chain which extends from Gaspé, Canada, to northern Georgia. The lofty range of the Smokies is the climax of the Appalachians and is the backbone of Great Smoky Mountains National Park.

Known as the cradle of eastern American vegetation, this area supplied plants and animals to the land exposed for the first time in thousands of years as the glacial ice sheet retreated northward. Primeval and timeworn as they are, vegetation densely covers the Smokies with a sea of green from base to summits, some rising more than 6,000 feet.

At first, the Great Smokies may appear to have a certain sameness, then suddenly the delight unfolds: The presence of junglelike plant life together with the prevalent haze charms many who visit the park. Wisps of fog rise from the valley as low-hanging clouds roll through the gaps following the summer rainstorms when most of the precipitation falls. Blue, cold water falls into rushing streams, tipping over the edges of stone after stone. A half-light hovers at the doorway to a mysterious, beckoning cave.

The mountains are steep, but not nearly unconquerable, faced with high rock, but not having the sheer face of the Tetons. Nature has mellowed the Great Smokies with time, gently filling deep valleys and rounding sharp peaks so that they have a graceful, undulating rhythm. The harshness has been worn away and replaced with placidity.

All this took time, 880 million years of it, before the Ice Age's glacial sheet covered the central United States down to the Ohio River, destroying all that lay before them. The Great Smoky Mountains escaped the earth-gnawing glaciers since they were beyond their reach and their climate an anathema to the masses of ice.

Gravel, sand and mud deposits first covered the region, the layers compressing the ones beneath until time and weight solidified them more than three miles thick. Then the land began to rise and side pressures caused the once-solid formations to break or buckle, forming faults in the surface. This disturbance affected much of North America.

Then the ice sheet destroyed and restricted much of the vegetation and animals around the Great Smoky Mountains. The region was at first refuge, then provider, when the ice retreated to the north, furnishing plant and animal life to the land which was raped.

As life began to spread outward from what is now part of the park, the rivers came and cut channels through the land mass, creating valleys in a haphazard pattern. The ages have done the rest, wearing away

The 600 miles of streams, including Little Pigeon River, add to the gentle scenic beauty of Great Smoky.

Located south of the Cades Cove loop road, the John Oliver cabin dates from 1818, when the veteran of the War of 1812 made his way across the Great Smokies to become the area's first permanent white settler.

mountain peaks, brushing away harsh corners and filling too-deep valleys with rock and silt so that vegetation might live and bring still more beauty to this ancient geological structure.

Most of the trees survived the rigorous climate to become the nucleus of deciduous trees which eventually spread and reforested the land with eastern hardwood trees.

There is no timberline; wide expanses of trees cover the hills with a mantle of green, shedding a fraction of their used vegetation each fall to build the humus for the enormous variety of flora for which the Smokies are noted.

Here are the broadleaved trees — yellow poplar, white ash, American beech, black cherry and northern red oak, growing below the mountain ash and red spruce in the cooler regions at higher altitudes. Surprisingly, the forests overlap because of environmental factors, but the spruce and fir stands are generally found in the Canadian zone above 5,000 feet.

The trees are a part of an ecological cycle existing because of the protection given the region by its national park status. Their life is interrelated with smaller plants, the rhododendron, ferns and a gamut of wildflowers. They, in turn, are links in the chain of survival for 50 species of mammals, 200 types of birds and fish hovering silently in deep stream-pools.

This country attracted settlers who were hardy, self-sufficient people mostly from Scotland and England. They vied for hunting and fishing lands with the Cherokee Indians whose reservation is now adjacent to the park on the south. The customs, speech and names of those pioneers cling to the region today.

Some of their descendants lived in Cades Cove, Tennessee, which was an isolated community until World War I and some of its citizens joined the armed services. It was seven years after the armistice before a good road linked this tiny town with the world around it. Today Cades Cove visitors can see the cabins and churches and the mill grinding cornmeal which was left when these mountain people sold their properties to the Government at the time the area became a national park.

Today, there are nearly 800 square miles for the people's pleasure in this region where all that is gentle and soft is supreme; a mass of green winter and summer, a climate kind to man, an abundant supply of water to nourish the natural treasures preserved in these venerable mountains.

Along Tennessee State Highway 73 flowers bloom in summer amid the trees that round the Great Smoky Mountains. A blue-green mist, for which the mountains were named, rises from the dense plant growth.

The fastidious raccoon begins a search for his dinner. He has his choice of over 70 kinds of fish including rainbow and brook trout.

A sunset at the 6,593-foot Mount Le Conte colors the early evening skies with a prism of color before the solitude of darkness begins.

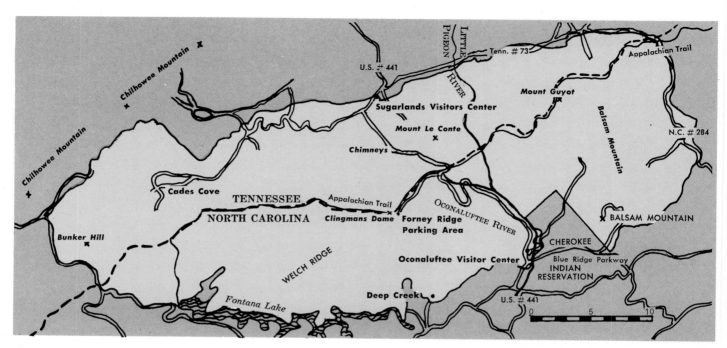

GREAT SMOKY MOUNTAINS NATIONAL PARK

*A*long the Appalachian Trail, which forms the border between Tennessee and North Carolina, is a point called Charlie's Bunion (opposite, above) commanding an excellent view of the park. The highest point of the intermountain route is Newfound Gap (opposite, below). The higher elevations in the park contain extensive stands of virgin red spruce. A rehabilitated cabin (left) is evidence of the settlers who lived quietly in this area well into the 20th century.

HALEAKALA

LOCATION: Hawaii
(Maui Island)
SIZE: 27,283 acres
ESTABLISHED: 1916

The land sleeps here now, resting under the warm Pacific sun after the long day geologists count in millions of years. To Haleakala (pronounced HA-lay-ah-kah-LA), it is night and a well-deserved rest, for this Hawaiian volcano helped form the lovely green fingers that probe the sea as part of our 50th state.

To Polynesians, it means "House of the Sun," and it was once that, belching forth angry torrents of fire and lava, making night as day, until it subsided in placid surrender to time, leaving as a heritage one of the showplaces of the National Park System so that all might understand the forces of geological evolution.

On a clear day — and there are many in the Pacific — the summit affords a spectacular view of the neighboring islands of Hawaii, Lanai, Molokai and occasionally Oahu. Turn the eyes a bit downward, and unfolding beyond the crater's rim is a vast hole in the earth, gouged by water erosion, leaving acres of symmetrical cinder cones painted with primeval colors huddled inside the great formations of cliffs whose tops are hidden in the moist clouds, lending even more vastness to the gigantic, dormant crater seven and a half miles long and two and a half miles wide.

Haleakala's history is shrouded in the still-growing science of geology, yet many scientists agree that this House of the Sun was once more than 11,000 feet high, a summit about 1,000 feet greater than the one we see now. She once slowed her volcanic eruptions,

Meaning "House of the Sun," Haleakala Crater (opposite) changes color almost hourly as the sun passes overhead, becoming most vivid at mid-afternoon. When viewed from the rim above Kapalaoa Cabin (above), hikers on the Sliding Sands Trail can see the 19-square mile crater floor 3,000 feet below the summit.

and water came to carve two deep valleys in opposite sides of the mountain which eventually met. Then, the fury of the subterranean eruptions began anew and lava flows cascaded into the valleys atop one another after their first outpourings reached the sea. The level of the valleys seen today is the height of the cooled, molten rock, save for a bit of topsoil created by time alone.

Cones of cinder were formed as high as 600 feet, and volcanic bombs and spatter spurted from fissures in the earth, propelled by supercharged gases. Eventually, a water-carved depression, one partially filled, was created, resembling a true volcanic crater. Until 1961, it was hidden by distance from the rest of Hawaii Volcanoes National Park, when it was made a singular attraction of the system because of its size.

The House of the Sun is quiet now, for no erup-tions have occurred here for centuries. But there is the appeal of something new, raw, a just-formed land, and in geological terms it is that. Lava is sterile stuff, for nothing can survive its heat. Generations of plant life have rained down upon the cooled rock until, in places, anyway, here and there a plant has been able to gain a foothold. That is fortunate, for they will flourish, then die, deepening the topsoil by a fraction of a millimeter so that other plants might follow eventually.

Life grows slowly at Haleakala National Park, for this is still a new land. But the silversword has fought grazing animals, man and the barren beds of lava to thrust its spheres of silvery, dagger-shaped leaves and three to seven-foot flowers, casting to the four winds thousands of seeds, then dying — the first handful of compost to fertilize the silent mountain.

*J*ound nowhere else in the world, the silversword (right) grows mostly in dry cinder areas in the crater or above 8,000 feet on the outer slopes. Despite its relation to sunflowers, it resembles a yucca. Hanakauhi (below), at 8,910 feet above sea level, is part of the crater's north rim. Within Haleakala Crater there are hundreds of cinder cones (below left), formed by ash spurted through their vents.

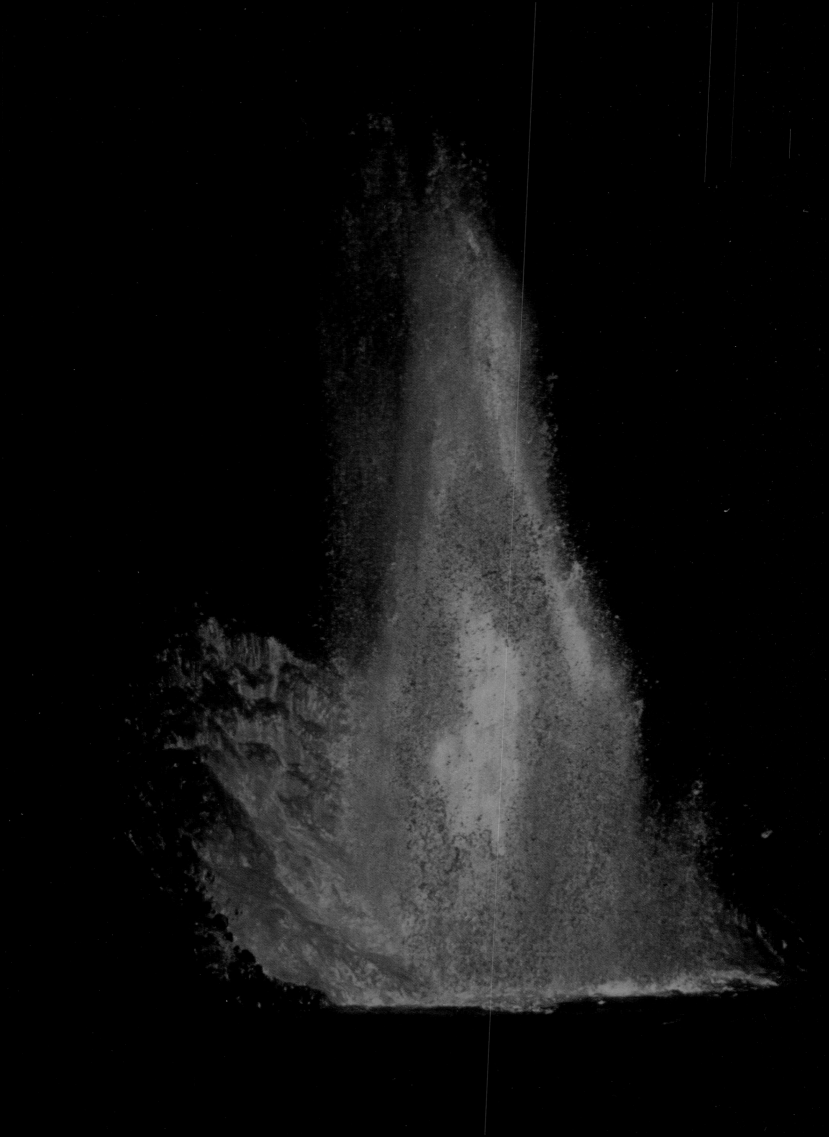

HAWAII VOLCANOES

LOCATION: Hawaii
(Hawaii Island)
SIZE: 220,345 acres
ESTABLISHED: 1916

Huge mountains, their gray, lifeless sides warmed by the Pacific sun, spout their anger at the placid blue seas around them, belching fountains of lava and red fire into the sky, pouring orange-red streams of molten rock down unresisting slopes.

This is a link with the past; geological history in the making as the Hawaiian Islands continue to emerge from the sea as they first did five to ten million years ago. Hawaii Island, largest of the chain, is the site of Mauna Loa, a 13,680-foot summit where Hawaii Volcanoes National Park begins, stretching southeast to the seacoast, a place of contrasts where umbrella-shaped palms and dense jungles of ferns lie near gaunt mountains and beside lava deserts.

The region has fascinated visitors for more than a century. The Rev. William Ellis, a British missionary, saw it in 1823 and said in his *A Tour Through Hawaii:* "... A spectacle, sublime and even appalling, presented itself before us. We stopped and trembled. Astonishment and awe for some moments rendered us mute.... The bottom was covered with lava, and the southwest and northern parts of it were one vast flood of burning matter, in a stage of terrific ebullition, rolling to and fro its 'fiery surge' and flaming billows."

The spectacle of the volcano, Kilauea, impressed Mr. Ellis and countless thousands since. Within the volcano at that time, at Halemaumau, was a great lake of rolling lava which spread across the floor, and

Effervescing several hundred feet, the lava fountain (left) is considered to be relatively gentle. Hawaii Volcanoes National Park has two of the most active volcanoes in the world. Restricted to the volcanic mountains of Hawaii Island is the rare Néne' or Hawaiian Goose (above), which is now on the verge of extinction.

at other times seeped into earth fissures to produce avalanches of fire. A later visitor stared at the sight, then told a guide, "I've seen hell. Now I want to go home." This "lava-lake" phase ceased with the steam explosion of 1924.

From the 11-mile Crater Rim Drive around the summit caldera of Kilauea volcano, Kilauea Crater, the visitor can see the destruction wrought by the forces of nature — cones of cinder, bluffs alive with steam and recent flows of lava. One of the most impressive sections is the "devastated area," which was denuded of vegetation during the 1959 eruption of Kilauea Iki. The ancient Hawaiians made a deity of Pele, the goddess of volcanoes, whom they believed lived in Halemaumau, Kilauea's most active vent. It was her wrath, they said, which caused the eruptions, destroying villages and tilled lands.

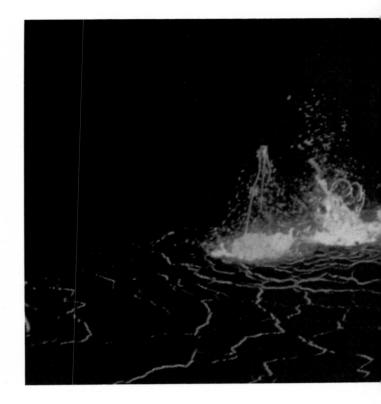

From the summit caldera, the visitor passes along the Chain of Craters, part of the east rift of the volcano where the road winds past deep craters in which eruptions have recently taken place. In March, 1965, a fissure on the side of Makaopuhi Crater poured forth a lake of lava almost 300 feet deep. During the 1959 eruption of Kilauea Iki, lava spewed more than 1,900 feet high, filling a crater with molten lava to a depth of about 400 feet. Until recently, the most spectacular of all volcanoes here was Mauna Loa, but it has not erupted since 1950.

From Makaopuhi Crater near the end of the chain, the island's newest scenic road passes along the southeast coast, past ancient villages and sites of religious temples. The mighty mountains of fire must have prompted these peoples to great religious fervor. At Wahaula Heiau near the eastern edge of the park is one of the island's best-known places of worship where it is reputed that one of the last human sacrifices was performed under the old religion.

Now the religion is appreciation of and humility before nature, which is protected within the boundaries of this park in a subtropical corner of paradise.

T he Gingerlily (bottom) is the flower used in leis in the Hawaiian Islands. Originally from India, it is the most romantic of the gingers, with petals like folded moth wings, and sometimes grows as high as seven feet. Small lava fountains (top) in a sea of molten lava are believed to begin 35 miles down within the earth's mantle. After filling a reservoir two miles beneath the surface, the lava works its way through fissures to erupt for as long as a month at the summit. In 1959 one fountain roared at 1,900 feet, highest ever witnessed, filling Kilauea Iki (right) 400 feet deep. Cool at the surface, it remains hot beneath.

Although Hot Springs National Park is famous for its medicinal waters, it has other attractions such as interesting scenery, horseback riding and camping.

HOT SPRINGS

LOCATION: Southwest-Central Arkansas
SIZE: 3,535 acres
ESTABLISHED: 1921

A few months before he died, Hernando de Soto, bold Spanish explorer and conquistador, passed through what is now Hot Springs and possibly bathed in its waters. He was searching for gold and he probably never got closer to his impossible dream than his immersion in the warm water which springs from vents in the gray, volcanic tuff at the base of Hot Springs Mountain near the center of Arkansas.

That was the year 1541. Before the arrival of the white man the Indian was reportedly attracted to these hot waters where the "Great Spirit" dwelled. The Dunbar and Hunter Expedition in 1804 mapped the water route from Natchez to the springs and made a chemical analysis of them. Soon after, a permanent settlement developed which by 1820 included an inn and several crude canvas-shack bathhouses. In 1832 Congress set aside the hot springs as a reservation, but without supervision for over 40 years.

Today's national park of 1,035 acres is visited annually by several hundred thousand tourists. The park's primary significance is probably that it is this country's most important example of man's centuries-old romance with and affinity for the thermal and mineral waters of the world. The magical liquid minerals boil and bubble up from the west slope at the base of Hot Springs Mountain in 47 springs with an average daily flow of almost a million gallons and an average temperature of 143 degrees Fahrenheit.

"The springs are now the property of the people," the superintendent of Government bathhouses wrote to the Secretary of the Interior in 1915. "They are

free from monopoly and extortion, and within the reach of all." Yet the area did not become a national park until 1921.

There is no certainty about what causes the hot springs. The currently favored theory is that the springs are formed when rainwater sinks into the ground between Sugarloaf and West Mountains, then rises along tilted layers of rock to emerge finally through the geological fault at the base of Hot Springs Mountain.

The heated water is variously attributed to inordinately deep and uncooled underground rock, chemical reactions near the bottom of the wells, friction from sliding rock masses at profound earth-depths or compression from overlying rock burden and radioactive minerals far beyond the range of the discerning instruments of geologists.

Not all visitors take the waters. Below the mountain is the gay winter resort city of Hot Springs where horse racing and golfing rival the waters. And in the park itself, one of the nation's oldest national preserves, are five rugged little mountains and oak-hickory-pine forests which consistently bring their own special rewards.

Perhaps the late President John F. Kennedy best summed up the twin beneficence of a preserve like Hot Springs when he declared in 1962: "We must have places where we can find release from the tensions of an increasingly industrialized civilization, where we can have personal contact with the natural environment which sustains us."

There is no certain explanation of the hot springs' mechanism, but the favored theory says the water is seeping rainwater, shown as icicles at Dripping Springs.

To show visitors what the springs looked like in a natural state, one of the 47 has been left open. The others are sealed to prevent outside contamination.

Two of the many moods of Isle Royale: (above) a tranquil beauty descends with night upon the numerous lakes and islands of the archipelago, while (right) man can find himself the isolated splendor that comes with being in the north woods, away from the mainland's daily routine of hurry and heaviness.

ISLE ROYALE

LOCATION: Michigan
(in Lake Superior)
SIZE: 539,341 acres
ESTABLISHED: 1940

Isle Royale, now north woods wilderness held in a lake's solitude, is visibly haunted by the grace and majesty of its geologic past. This handsomely endowed protectorate of vast Lake Superior, in Michigan, and 22 miles from the Minnesota shore, is enveloped by the greatest of the Great Lakes, the lake which marks the site of the southern end of an ancient and possibly one of the highest mountain ranges that ever existed on our continent.

The formation of Lake Superior and perhaps Isle Royale itself is explained eloquently by Rutherford Platt in *The Great American Forest:* "Through timeless eras . . . in many places the uplift of mountains so weakened the edge of the Canadian Shield [a shield is a broad, massive, symmetrical rock upheaval] that it gave way, . . . creating depressions for future lakes and river valleys."

The pure copper deposits of Isle Royale and even the mineral riches of its geologic cousin the Mesabi Range are explained by Platt: "The Canadian Shield became the pedestal of the North Woods." He describes the intrusions of plutonic minerals and the ravaging of the area's surface by glaciers, the outcroppings of rock in which, on Isle Royale itself, the Indians found copper "so pure it can be used without smelting. This was the source of copper for Indian artifacts found scattered far and wide through the American wilderness."

Isle Royale, 45 miles in length, is redolent with the ancient history of Indian copper miners, who reportedly worked there 4,000 years ago. Its fjord-like harbors, sheltered bays and interior, parallel ridges attaining a height of 700 feet, were first looked upon by white men in 1699. These were heroic French explorers who named the island for Louis XIV.

Yet white men did not recognize that although the copper of Isle Royale was satisfactory for the primitive artisan, it wasn't in sufficient concentration for modern industrial needs. Miners ventured across the lake in the 1840's and 1870's, but by 1900 their mines were abandoned.

The canoe yielded to the motor launch, the small boat to the excursion vessel. Hotels and summer homes were beginning to multiply. A cry was raised and the administration of the second great conservationist Roosevelt responded to their reasoned pleas. In 1936, Franklin Delano Roosevelt signed the Isle Royale National Park Act resulting in its establishment four years later.

Two hundred tiny islands and countless rocks, inviting water explorers, surround the main island; thus the entire park area can be called an archipelago. A coniferous sweep of trees covers the northeast and perimeter of the island, and maple-birch hardwoods dominate the higher interior. Bald ridges, bogs, spruce and cedar swamps dot the landscape, offering additional havens for the water birds.

"The muzzles of moose cut sliding V's on the mirrors of the ponds," as Rutherford Platt suggests of the north woods area. On Isle Royale approximately 600 of the long-legged, antlered beasts form the relatively large population.

Beavers, red foxes, snowshoe hares, red squirrels find refuge and sustenance here. The lonely cry of the loon, the din of the herring gull, the scream of the bald eagle are heard on the island reaches.

There are no roads on the island. The hiker and canoeist, however, can maneuver here with more than 120 miles of trails to be negotiated amid the wild splendor, although they should remember that the nights are cool and even day temperatures seldom rise above 80 degrees. Many small boats are handy to the seeker of water worlds at Rock Harbor and Windigo. Fishermen call the island "the pike capital of the nation" because of the abundance of pike in the 200 lakes and ponds. Isle Royale is the north woods in autonomous compactness, with fascination for all.

Moose (left), while common at Isle Royale, did not come until 1912 when Lake Superior froze across to Canada, 15 miles away. They eat water plants, leaves and twigs. At the Middle Islands Entrance to Rock Harbor stands the Old Rock Harbor Lighthouse (above). Rock Harbor, longest of the four main harbors, is typical of the primitive, but exciting American scenery found at Isle Royale (upper right). Very common to Isle Royale is the largest rodent in the United States, the beaver (lower right). The beaver is the engineer of the wild, the only mammal, beside humans, that alters its environment to suit its needs. Most active at dusk and dawn, the beaver builds and repairs dams, lodges and canals.

LASSEN VOLCANIC

LOCATION: Northeastern California
SIZE: 106,934 acres
ESTABLISHED: 1916

Lassen Peak, reflected in a nearby lake, stands at the southern end of the Cascade Range. The largest plug dome volcano in the world dominates the park, a park that offers both scenic beauty and geologic interest because of its extensive volcanic past.

In the order of nature, often where there is chaos, great beauty is nearby.

This seems to be particularly true of the lush, sylvan beauty that neighbors on volcanoes in Italy, the South Sea Islands, South America and, in our own country, Lassen Volcanic National Park of northeastern California. For where volcanoes are, active or inactive, the slopes and lowlands of the tumultuous mountains are usually rich with the resources that satisfy the physical and spiritual needs of man: food and drink for his body, shelter for his family.

Lassen Peak, once called San Jose by Spanish explorers, is now an inactive plug dome volcano. But it was once considered the only active volcano in the United States, having erupted as recently as 1914 and 1915, remaining fire-breathing and occasionally rumbling until 1921.

The 10,457-foot peak was the habitat and wonderment of four tribes of Indians long before Spaniard Luis Arguillo discovered it in 1821. This once fierce, lava-spewing mountain in the Cascade Range, not far from the Sierra Nevada, served as a territorial monument, dividing the regions of the Atsugewi, Maidu, Yana and Yahi, who foraged in its vicinity and lived in harmony around its slopes. In the park, also, the true American natives must have known the fearsome majesty of other volcanic heights now called Cinder Cone, Bumpass Hell and Devils Kitchen.

Now, as then, coniferous forests, flower-blanketed mountain meadows, sun-glinting and tree-shadowy lakes and streams characterize the 165 square mile area. Deer are abundant in the fields of summer; over 150 species of birds beautify the foliage; golden-mantled ground squirrels, chipmunks, red squirrels, bear are permanent tenants.

The view from Lassen Park Road, extending from the southwestern to northwestern corner of the park,

Lassen Park Road (California 89) meanders past the major interest sites of Lassen Volcanic National Park.

and half encircling the base of Lassen Peak, is stunningly comprehensive. Yet the leisurely assimilation of the park's beauty and bizarre landmarks appeals more to the view from behind a walking stick than through an automobile windshield. It is a hiker's and camper's park, demanding the effort, and offering scenic rewards not accessible to the automobile. The 150 miles of trails are highlighted by the path which leads to Bumpass Hell, a 16-acre tract of boiling, sulphurous springs, named after K. V. Bumpass who discovered it in 1864.

The peak, the park, the surrounding national forest and a county, all are named after Peter Lassen, a Danish immigrant blacksmith, who familiarized himself and others with the area in the 1830's. He early acquired a large parcel of land at Vina, California. During the Gold Rush he guided migrants across these mountains from the East, into the Sacramento Valley. He used the peak as a storied landmark and his rancho as a hostel. Thus, the bestowal of his name on specific points and general area, by the U.S. Geographic Board in 1915.

Lassen's trail, however, did not wind into the area now included in the park. W. H. Nobles crossed through the northern part of the present expanse from Butte Lake to Manzanita Lake in 1852. Nobles' route was considered a more direct approach to the Sacramento Valley.

Lassen Peak and Cinder Cone were designated as national monuments on May 6, 1907. The eruptions in 1914 and 1915 electrified public interest in the American volcano and expedited the park's establishment on August 9, 1916. Here is a park and peak which Associate Supreme Court Justice, William O. Douglas, must have had in mind when he wrote that some people "must find a peak or a ridge that they can reach under their own power alone."

Bumpass Hell, where steam rises from boiling mudpots, indicates that Lassen may be dormant but not extinct.

MAMMOTH CAVE

The darkness grips the visitor, then the depths slowly come into focus as the eyes adjust themselves to the underworld of Kentucky's Mammoth Cave, which has been a lure to awestruck men since it was first trod by primitives.

It is still a place of mystery, this partially unexplored hollow land beneath the surface. The ancients braved superstition and penetrated more than three miles of its vaulted passages, seeking gypsum. The dry, even temperatured air has preserved for centuries their worn-out sandals and burnt torch ends, scattered here and there among footprints before sheer walls hacked with rude stone tools. Why they sought the soft mineral is not known. The remains of one of them is still there, his body mummified after he was crushed by a six-ton boulder while gathering the stone 2,400 years ago.

The yawning cavern was rediscovered by an unknown white man in 1798, and a few years later by another seeking saltpeter, or potassium nitrate, a prime ingredient of black gunpowder. The bored-out tree trunks used to carry the chemical solution to vats are still here, along with other well-preserved artifacts of the operation.

The saltpeter industry died after the War of 1812; then began Mammoth Cave's career as a tourist attraction, although much of it remained unexplored. Jenny Lind sang here, her voice echoing and reechoing through the rooms of stone. Edwin Booth, the great Shakespearian actor, intoned the philosophy of Hamlet in this apt surrounding and Grand Duke Alexis of Russia paid the cave a visit along with thousands of others who linked it with Niagara Falls as a great attraction.

In 1837 a 15-year-old boy named Stephen Bishop, among the cave's first guides, crossed the Bottomless Pit on a slender pole, opening the way to extensive uncharted corridors and passages. Bishop guided the many eminent scientists who visited the cave there-

LOCATION: Southwest-Central Kentucky
SIZE: 51,354 acres
ESTABLISHED: 1941

Iron oxide in the calcium carbonate gives the Golden Fleece (left) in Mammoth Cave its golden color. The Hindu Temple (above) displays many varied cave formations: stalactites, stalagmites and columns.

after, and achieved world renown before he died in 1859. He is buried in what is now the park. Later the cave became an underground tuberculosis sanitarium. It was proposed as a national park in 1911, but that wasn't accomplished until 30 years later.

The cave is a maze of corridors connecting huge, domed chambers and deep pits. They were formed 340 million years ago when the limestone was the bed of an ancient sea. The land rose, and water inched into the rock, eroding the giant passages seen today. The formations have quaint, picturesque names — Fat Man's Misery, a narrow channel out into the floor of a large room; Frozen Niagara; the Snowball Room. Among the half-dozen guided tours available in Mammoth Cave is a boat ride on Echo River, the world's best-known underground stream. Nearly a million persons a year visit this great natural wonder.

Above ground, two lovely rivers flow through the park, winding past deep green forests and a blaze of colorful wildflowers, a strange paradox to the weird, wonderful world spread out, down below.

*B*lindfish (left), which inhabit the subterranean Echo River, have developed acute senses of touch and smell. They are small, colorless and translucent. Stalactites and stalagmites form rigid columns in the Lion's Cage (above left). During the War of 1812, the Rotunda (above) was used to mine saltpeter. This huge room is one of Mammoth Cave's largest. Onyx stalactites combine to make the Drapery Room, a popular sight at Mammoth Cave National Park.

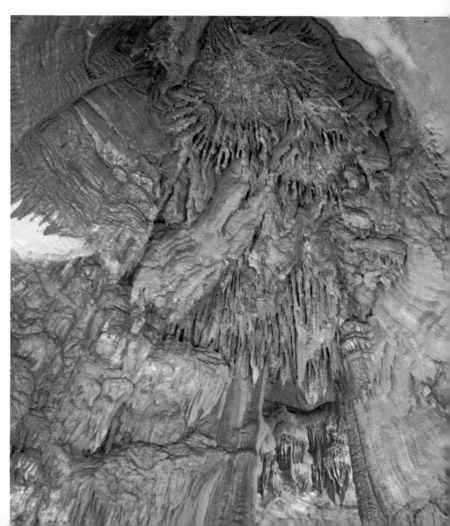

MESA VERDE

LOCATION: Southwestern Colorado
SIZE: 52,074 acres
ESTABLISHED: 1906

About 250 years before conquistador Coronado's ruthless and romanticized quest in 1540 through Arizona and New Mexico, seeking the illusory wealth of the "Seven Cities of Cibola," the cliff-dwelling Indians of southwestern Colorado's Mesa Verde had disappeared into archeological history.

For 800 years the Indians of the Four Corners country cultivated their beans and maize, lived and prospered — then vanished.

The empty homes of these departed people remain behind today, preserved in protective rock-shelters by the mild climate of this country. Those who come today to wonder at the majesty of Cliff Palace, the largest cliff dwelling of them all, must feel much as the cowboys did in the late 19th century when they stumbled onto it while looking for grazing cattle from atop the mesa.

News of the discoveries spread rapidly, and before long a great many curious people began to wander among the ruins, ferreting out their secrets. Unfortunately these people included careless tourists and callous curio-seekers, and some serious damage to the ruins resulted. Even though this was not an altogether bright period in the history of the Mesa Verde, the work of these early explorers began to attract the attention of more serious scholars. One of these was Gustaf Nordenskiold, a Swedish scientist who in 1891 directed the first scientific excavations in several of the cliff dwellings and published his findings. By 1900 a women's organization, the Colorado Cliff Dwellings Association, was incorporated and began working for the preservation of the ancient buildings. In 1906 their efforts attained fruition and Mesa Verde National Park was established by act of Congress on June 29. One result of this act is a regulation stating that all visitors to cliff dwellings must be accompanied by a National Park Service employee.

So successful has been the excavation and repair of the early damage to these precipitous Indian mansions that Cliff Palace, Balcony House and Spruce Tree House are now considered to be the best examples of cliff dwellings to be found in the continental United States. These citadels of man, built like the eagle's aerie in inaccessibility to enemy attack from below, are an everlasting tribute to how primitive man mastered the enduring craft of masonry.

In the Mesa Verde museum are restored fragile artifacts of cookery, agriculture, jewelry and pottery

The imposing Square Tower House (right), dating from the 11th century, was discovered by settlers in 1888.

which tell the history of a vanished cliff-dwelling civilization in graphic detail.

Although the story of Indian life on the Mesa Verde has been preserved so clearly, the sudden departure of these people from their homeland remains a mystery. As one gazes at the cliff dwellings, perched in the cliffs high above the canyon floors, they may seem to him impregnable castles, often guarded by towers. Perhaps a persistent enemy finally overran the farmers of the mesa, but there are other possibilities. The narrower growth of tree-rings in the late 13th century suggests to some that drought may have driven the Indians from this region. It may be that after 800 years of farming the mesa tops the Indians had exhausted the soils. Nevertheless the visitor who lets his imagination play over the spectacle of the cliff houses generally departs with a memory of the defensive refuges of a harassed people.

The quest for clues to these ancient people continues. The mystery may soon be solved in concrete scientific analysis. The National Park Service recently completed a five-year archeological study of Wetherill Mesa in the undeveloped western section of the park and possibly will come up with certain key answers.

When the new area under study is opened to the public, the number of cliff dwellings accessible to tourists, archeologists and anthropologists will double. Long House, Mug House and Step House specifically will be added to the park's houses of ancient wonder. And a new museum on Wetherill Mesa will fill out the gradually focusing jigsaw puzzle which gives us a quaint, unique, historical picture of a vanished American people.

The 400,000 people who visit Mesa Verde annually are thus given an extraordinary opportunity to be grateful for the forces of preservation and conservation which enable them to reflect on both the intrinsic perishability and immortality which is the life and time of man.

Shadows move across Mesa Verde plateau country (right) as 9,884-foot Ute Peak stands snowcapped in the distance. The Sun Temple (opposite, above), a mesa-top ceremonial structure, was built about 1200 A.D. near Fewkes Canyon. Under summer clouds, the La Plata Mountains provide a background for scenic views along Mesa Verde park road (opposite, below).

*A*ncient masonry forms are viewed through a doorway at Spruce Tree House (below left), the best preserved large cliff dwelling. A diorama of Spruce Tree House (left) in the park museum depicts the daily life of the Pueblo villagers. The Cliff Palace (below) is the most extensive of the park's cliff dwellings. The circular ceremonial chambers near the living areas were central features of the Pueblo culture.

MOUNT McKINLEY

The Wilderness of Denali is not tamed. It is raw and primal, and a man feels very small in it. Almost anywhere off the one road he is truly alone—and sometimes a little afraid.

It is a vast land, which dwarfs normal scales. Sprawling river bars, peopled with the swarming specks that are the caribou, wind out of immensity at the foot of the hills. The wind across the tundra is clean, untainted by mankind.

The spirit of the wolf hangs over the land. Unseen, his presence is felt. He is the warden and unwitting benefactor of the caribou, the superb culmination of the biotic pyramid—and the personification of the wild.

Over all, the Alaska Range rises in a succession of brilliant ridges, cornices, peaks—each magnificent in its own right, but nearly lost in the greater picture. Higher they rise, leading the eye to the massive upsurge that is *The Mountain*. A full three vertical miles above the living tundra soars its peak.

Nothing lives on the mountain, but the mountain lives. Avalanches leap from its walls. Seracs crash; glaciers rumble and grind. Clouds swirl about its flanks, and a snow plume is torn by the wind from its uppermost crests. In the evening, the glare of the eternal ice softens, glows with the color of fireweed, then pales to ivory against the darkened sky.

No one knows what white man saw the country first. Russian traders knew the mountain, called it *Bulshaia Gora,* or "Big Mountain." Early prospectors knew it as Densmore's Mountain. The Indians of the area had perhaps the most beautiful and fitting name of all: "Denali," "The High One."

But it was a young prospector, W. A. Dickey, who

LOCATION: South-Central Alaska
SIZE: 1,939,493 acres
ESTABLISHED: 1917

A subarctic wilderness at summer sunset (opposite): Wonder Lake and Mount McKinley, which at 20,320 feet is North America's highest peak. It is 250 miles south of Arctic Circle. Caribou (above), which are seen along the park road, are unique to Mount McKinley in the park system.

Among the park's many mountain glaciers is Muldrow Glacier. Some glaciers are 30 to 40 miles long.

realized the importance of the 20,320-foot peak in 1896, and named it after the champion of the gold standard, President William McKinley.

It is fortunate that one of the earliest explorers of the area was a naturalist and conservationist. Charles Sheldon, hunting specimens for the National Museum, roamed the country for three years, and felt its impact. Recognizing the intrinsic value of the landscape and its wildlife, he conceived the idea of making the area a national park while camping there in the summer of 1906. His vigorous efforts to create a refuge for the swarming wildlife, aided by the Boone and Crockett Club, brought about the establishment of Mount McKinley National Park just eleven years later. Today it is the only Park Service area which harbors the white Dall sheep and the barren grounds caribou, and its 3,030 square miles embrace more untouched wilderness than any other national park.

Mountaineers answered the challenge of Mount McKinley early. On April 6, 1910, a hardy group of sourdoughs climbed to the summit of the north peak of McKinley, carrying with them a 14-foot spruce pole. It was an astonishing feat, for the group was inexperienced and poorly equipped. Modern mountaineers find the climb as dangerous and demanding as a Himalayan expedition, but each year a few manage to stand atop the continent.

Relatively little has changed since Sheldon fought to make this area a park. A single graveled road winds its leisurely way 86 miles into the park, climbing from the deep green spruce of the taiga to the sweeping tapestry of the alpine tundra. You may see from the road the same wild peaks and teeming wildlife that

The Teklanika River flows down from the Alaska Range through a broad gravel bed near park road.

thrilled the first visitors. Over the tundra range groups of caribou, the bulls in late summer bearing brilliant white capes and towering, blood-red antlers. Moose, looking shiny black at a little distance, feed knee-deep in ponds or browse in willow thickets.

The deceptively lethargic-looking grizzly keeps his head down, gobbling berries, roots and grasses. Red foxes trot across the road, seemingly indifferent to man. Ptarmigan erupt into the air with a humorous, guttural croaking, their white wings flashing in startling contrast to their barred brown bodies.

In the ponds everywhere beavers are busy cutting willow. Golden eagles soar above. Gyrfalcons are sometimes seen, and marsh hawks swoop low across the dry flats. On the lower peaks, a spray of white dots becomes a flock of Dall sheep.

If you are very lucky, you may see a wolf. When you have seen the eyes of the wolf, you have seen the quintessence of wildness.

The park is generally accessible from June through the middle of September. In June and July the area is confronted with one of its few disadvantages—mosquitoes, which come after the late spring that leaves patches of snow at lower elevations even into June. During these same months there are 18 hours of sunlight daily and only semidarkness in the remaining hours. Although the winters are cold, snow depths seldom exceed three feet on the level at lower elevations.

Whatever the season, the mountain, once seen, even if its persistent shroud of clouds allows only a momentary view, becomes an indelible recollection. The wildness of the park, once experienced, even if at some distance, leaves its mark on a man.

MOUNT RAINIER

LOCATION: West-Central Washington
SIZE: 241,781 acres
ESTABLISHED: 1899

A rocky hiking trail winding up Pinnacle Peak offers a dramatic view of 14,410-foot Mount Rainier. Below the cloud line, the massive ice of the Nisqually Glacier inches slowly through a valley near Paradise, a mile-high visitor recreation area.

Rainier stands like a silent sentinel over the Cascade Range, a color covering of blue and green and tones of gray, clad in the white cap of cold and age, a garment which belies its fiery parentage.

The mountain soars above the Cascade Mountains of west-central Washington, rising 14,410 feet above sea level, her size so ponderous she covers a quarter of the national park's almost 380 square miles.

Deep, green stands of trees, alpine lakes, the diamond-tipped rush of icy water crashing over smooth boulders, delicate flowers hidden in shady glens, sprawling wild flower meadows — all are subdued by the spectacle of ice, laced like a child's finger painting across the faces of Mount Rainier. It has the greatest expanse of glaciers — about 40 in number — found in the United States outside of Alaska.

Rainier, part of that once-spectacular circle of volcanic activity which rings the Pacific from the Americas to Asia, was not always so placid, so gently touched or so green. Volcanic eruptions flowed lava upon lava, cinders upon ash, until the mountain grew with a fury nuclear energy cannot match. The Cascades to the east were created in the same manner, but Rainier retains more than a casual birthmark. At the summit are three peaks; Columbia Crest to the east is the highest, then two smaller but obvious volcanic craters. The summit craters on Columbia Crest, the mountain's high point, retain small vents which whisper steam into the thin air, melting the snow which lies about.

Now Rainier is quiet. Time, water and glaciers have worn great canyons and raised ridges along its once-smooth sides, and glaciers now spread across its body, square mile after square mile of slowly flowing ice, an active reminder of the natural forces which helped shape much of our landscape today.

One of them, the Emmons, measures over four miles long and a mile wide, built as the others by the incessant falls of snow, as much as 50 feet a year, packing layers upon layers until it is compressed by its own weight and begins to slide slowly downward. The water melts as it reaches lower elevations, but above, the tail of the glacier is always being formed so that the rushing rivers and stone-pounding streams below might have strength forever.

The water is the beginning of the various forms of natural life, irrigating lowland forests and alpine meadows. Douglas firs, western hemlocks and red cedars tower above the brown-needled floor where beams of sunlight break through and give life to Oregon grape, western sword fern, bunchberry, dogwood and soft, green mosses.

Beyond the forests lie patches of green meadows, threaded by foot trails and sprinkled with a rolling panorama of wild flowers: the avalanche fawnlily, yellow lambstongue fawnlily, western pasqueflower, marshmarigold and mountain buttercup bursting into bloom with the last snow melting. The Indian paintbrush, spikes of lupines, speedwell, valerian and American bistort fill the voids in August when the seeds of the spring flowers have been sown by the four winds to bloom again another year.

Apparently oblivious to Mount Rainier are the birds, 130 species of them, and half a hundred mammals — mule deer, black bear, elk and mountain goat, raccoons, squirrels and chipmunks — feeding in this horn of quiet plenty.

High above are plants stunted by the cold and elevation, grasping rocks and their roots seeking paper-thin fissures that nourishment might be found. The visitor here has taken a botanical "trip" far into Canada, for Hudson Bay is where this flora is generally displayed.

The snow which feeds Mount Rainier's glaciers originates as clouds over the Pacific Ocean. As the moisture-laden, westerly winds move inland, the first barrier they meet is the Cascade Range. Rising to pass over the mountains, they are cooled, and the condensing moisture falls as rain and snow. The heaviest precipitation falls on the windward slope, especially between 5,000 and 10,000 feet. Paradise Park receives about 100 inches in a year.

For all its beauty, Rainier must have been a forbidding scene to the Indians, since none of the dozen nations that visited the region is believed to have established permanent settlements. The mountain, an object of worship to some, was a hunting ground for others.

While some of the early tribes — the Nisqually, Cowlitz, Yakima and Klickitat — picked berries here in summer months, most probably feared the mountain. The deity who sent fire and molten rock through the top of a mountain was an unfriendly being, as early explorers seeking guides soon found.

Captain George Vancouver of the Royal Navy is

The nature-sculptured ice caves under the Paradise Glacier are known for their glistening illumination.

thought to be the first white man to see the mountain. On May 8, 1792, while on a journey of exploration for the British government, he wrote: "The weather was serene and pleasant, and the country continued to exhibit between us and the eastern snowy range the same luxuriant appearance. At its northern extremity, Mount Baker bore by compass North 22 East; the round, snowy mountain, now forming its southern extremity and which, after my friend, Rear Admiral Rainier, I distinguished by the name of Mount Rainier. . . ."

Tolmie Peak was named for the young Scots physician, William Fraser Tolmie, employed by Hudson Bay Company, who left Fort Nisqually in August, 1833. A few days later he climbed to the "summit of a snowy peak immediately under Mount Rainier."

It was later christened for him. Dr. Tolmie's name is also found in a creek and in the Tolmie saxifrage, a common plant growing in the park's upper regions.

Rainier itself stood unconquered for years. The first attempt in 1857 failed, and it was not until August 17, 1870, that Hazard Stevens and P. B. Van Trump reached the summit. Thirteen years later, James Longmire developed a small part of what is now the park after he discovered mineral springs.

Clouds and fog often obscure the mountain. There is, however, usually warm, clear weather from about July 1 to mid-September. In many years, Indian summer weather continues well into October, when autumn colors bring out still another kind of quality possessed by this magnificent mountain and the land that surrounds it.

*M*ount Rainier (above) stands between layers of pale color at dusk. Moisture laden clouds sweep in from the Pacific Ocean in changing patterns over the mountain. Among the many wildflowers in the park is the western anemone (right), a perennial herb found in mountain valleys. Green fir tree spires (far right) rise from the forest floor at Eunice Lake, near Tolmie Peak in the park's northwestern corner.

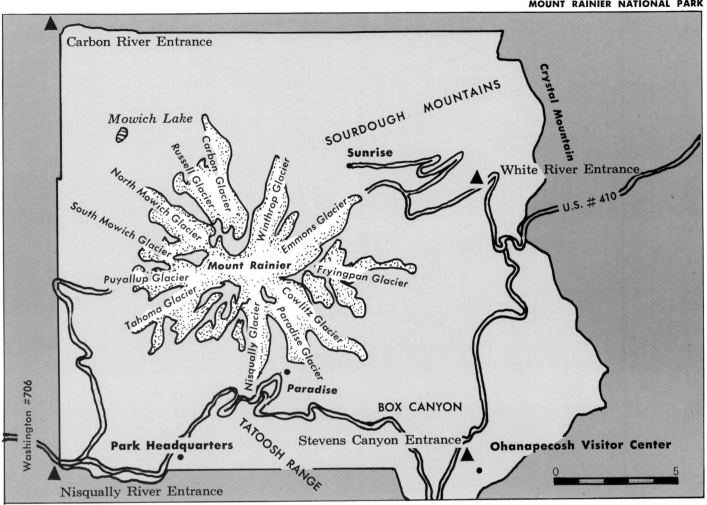

Carbon River Entrance

Mowich Lake

Carbon Glacier

Russell Glacier

North Mowich Glacier

South Mowich Glacier

Winthrop Glacier

SOURDOUGH MOUNTAINS

Sunrise

Crystal Mountain

White River Entrance

U.S. # 410

Emmons Glacier

Mount Rainier

Fryingpan Glacier

Puyallup Glacier

Tahoma Glacier

Cowlitz Glacier

Paradise Glacier

Nisqually Glacier

Paradise

BOX CANYON

Washington #706

Park Headquarters

TATOOSH RANGE

Stevens Canyon Entrance

Ohanapecosh Visitor Center

Nisqually River Entrance

0   5

*G*lacial movement, heavy snowfall and swirling winds create a changing terrain for mountaineers and skiers. A ski-climbing party passes a Camp Muir marker (opposite, below) as the sun silhouettes Mount Adams in the distance. Alpine snowfields (opposite, above) erode into low ridges under a sharp, carving wind. Ice breakups on Cowlitz Glacier (above left) and a sheer cliff face on Pinnacle Peak (above right) provide a challenge for climbers. From Sunrise (overleaf), the mountain looms skyward.

At Olympic National Park, in Washington, the civilization of man defers almost totally to the civilization of the tree. Amid these thousands of acres of mountain and coastal wilderness, 50 miles wide and 200 miles in circumference, the tropical-like luxuriance of rain forests vies in beauty and splendor with the majestic eminence of an immense conifer empire on primeval coasts and on the flanks of soaring peaks.

Such is man's deferment to this almost preternatural infinitude of green — the hushed, eternal realm of the Sitka spruce, western hemlock, Douglas-fir and red cedar, among others — that park trail crews often cut narrow, wandering foot trails through the wilderness. In the forest depths abound the natural civilization of wildlife and wildflowers — the animals, birds, and both familiar and exotic blooms, which flourish in a protective privacy redolent of the legendary preserves of Adam and Eve.

Fifty-six species of wild mammals inhabit Olympic Park, with some of their more migratory marine members ranging from season to season along the coastline from Alaska, through British Columbia and Washington State, to Lower California, over a distance of 4,000 miles. Around 6,000 "Roosevelt" elk (also called American elk or wapiti) live in the park and can be glimpsed moving toward the high country in the summer. More prominent residents also include the black-tailed deer and Olympic marmot, with mountain goat, bear, raccoons, mink, otter and mountain beaver quick and alive to the alert glance of the amateur naturalist. About 140 kinds of birds await the reverence and keen eye of the "watchers" with eagles, ravens, hawks, more discernible along the wild seacoast and among the craggy heights of the park.

Riots of wildflowers carpet the alpine meadows around Mt. Olympus, 7,965 feet high, and the other peaks, several of which rise above 7,000 feet. Of Olympic Park's wildflower life E. B. Webster said in his book, *The Friendly Mountain:* "Flowers of every shape and hue. Flowers standing shoulder to shoulder, as thick as daisies in a pasture, or clover in the field. Red columbine, yellow and blue asters, scarlet paint brushes, blue lupine, white valerian . . . all thrown

OLYMPIC

LOCATION: Northwestern Washington
SIZE: 896,599 acres
ESTABLISHED: 1938

Olympic presents two distinct topographical faces to the visitor, glacier-formed mountains and rugged sea coast. Rocky marine monoliths and seaweathered driftwood enhance Olympic National Park's 50 miles of Pacific Ocean beaches.

together in one gorgeous blanket of thoroughly mixed color."

The Strait of Juan de Fuca separates the park area from Canada. In 1774 the Spanish sea captain Juan Perez sailed through these waters of splendor, discovering the Olympic Mountains and originally calling them El Cerro de la Santa Rosalia. It remained for Capt. John Meares of Great Britain to explore the area in 1778 during which he named the highest peak "Mount Olympus," a designation later charted by Capt. George Vancouver.

Pacific Ocean tides break, ebb and flow against the park's western shoreline. Eastward, Puget Sound and Hood Canal form the added gift of isolation, separating, with salt water barriers, the peninsula and mainland of Washington State.

Along the fascinating shores, isolated conifers, twisted and misshapen, dot the shorelines. Then the fragmented shore, the home of the seal and wildfowl life of the sea, yields to sheer cliffs, fog-shrouded or sparkling in the sun, depending upon the day's weather. This massive moisture-channeling, aided by 142 inches of annual rainfall nourishes, on the western side, the finest remains of the Pacific Northwest rain forests.

The overwhelming impression of the rain forest is in Andrew Marvell's phrase: "a green lamp in a green shade." Or as one park service man said: "When one is inside the forest and the sun comes out, it is like being inside a giant emerald." Here, giant cone-bearing trees rise to nearly 300 feet above the forest floor. Red alders and black cottonwoods edge the stream banks where cutthroat, rainbow and brook trout thrive and steelhead seek the secluded streams in winter.

The lordly conifers dominate the realm, but here in the rain forest, the lesser fiefdoms of the tree kingdom are big-leaved and slender vine maples, burdened into arches by heavy veils of clubmoss. Most of this subsidiary civilization of the tree flourishes in openings under the dense conifer canopy. In the valleys of the Hoh, Quinault and Queets Rivers, the wondrous renewal process of future growth continues interminably as spongy, rotting undergrowth returns the nutrients to the soil where new tree life is nourished.

The disappearance of the great rain forests, which once covered a coastal area from northern California to southern Alaska, highlights the preciousness of this magnificent "remnant" in Olympic National Park. It is almost as if a splendid tropical jungle lies at the foot of the more typically Northwestern snow-covered peaks which pierce the clouds at elevations of 3,000 to 8,000 feet. Majestic Mt. Olympus dominates the uplands where more than 60 glaciers grow and recede, and these 25 square miles of ice hone down the mountains in the slow, eternal movement of time.

This mountainous interior lay unexplored until the winter of 1889-1890 when James H. Christie led the *Seattle Press* Expedition on the first crossing from Port Angeles to the Pacific Ocean. That summer, Lt. Joseph P. O'Neil led another expedition, crossing the mountains from Hood Canal to the Pacific.

Lt. O'Neil was the first to propose that the mountains would "serve admirably for a national park." A first step occurred in 1897 when President Cleveland created the Olympic Forest Reserve. A portion of the reserve was set aside as Mt. Olympus National Monument by that champion of outdoor life, President Theodore Roosevelt, in 1909. The long struggle for the permanent preservation of this vast retreat of nature ended on June 29, 1938, when Olympic National Park was established under another Roosevelt, F.D.R. Further land additions were made in 1940, 1943 and 1953, expanding the park to its authorized expanse of nearly 1,400 square miles.

The park enjoys its most favorable weather in the summer and early autumn. Although impassable snows close the higher elevations from late fall to early spring, a road is kept open, Christmas through March, from Port Angeles to the weekend ski area at Hurricane Ridge. The high-country roads and trails are usually free of snow by July.

The park's many peaks challenge both the experienced and amateur mountain climber. During June, July and August, when all 14 roads that enter the park are open, hikers and horsemen explore more than 600 miles of trails except for portions of high country where barriers of immutable snow confront the venturesome.

This is Olympic Park, a gigantic, precious gem in the diadem of America's natural beauty, stretching from coast to coast. Here, still, the conifer is supreme, symbolized by the royal Sitka spruce, with needles hard and sharp as steel, sentinel of mountain and sea, spilling the wind in a sustained whisper, or twanging its branches in the brunt of the sea blast.

Spring in Olympic is marked by the pink rhododendron, the official flower of the State of Washington.

*R*oped together for safety, mountain climbers pass craggy Blue Glacier (left) on 7,965-foot Mount Olympus, the park's highest peak. A less strenuous climb to high elevation is offered by the automobile road and nature trails at panoramic Hurricane Ridge (above left). Deep crevices ridge Blue Glacier (above), creating a spectacular setting for cross-ice pack hikes by well-equipped, seasoned climbers.

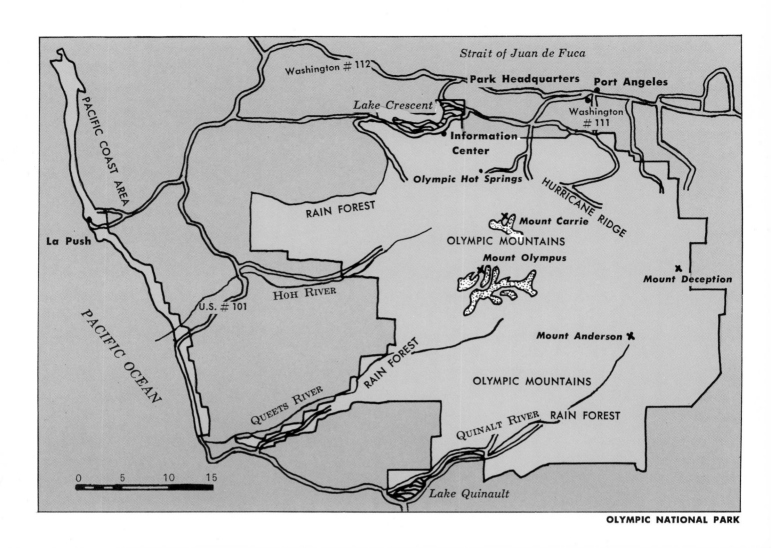

OLYMPIC NATIONAL PARK

Maritime fog climbs to the steep sides of snow-crowned Bailey Range (left) near the Strait of Juan de Fuca on the park's northeastern edge. At the opposite side of Olympic, the highest amount of annual rainfall in the United States creates yellow-green rain forests (above), a unique combination of towering conifers, smaller moss-covered vine maples, sword-like ferns and soft ground cover.

Mountain and valley vistas at Deer Park (above left) on Olympic's northeastern corner create a setting for visitor solitude. A common American wildflower, the tiger lily (right), finds an alpine home in a meadow at Hurricane Ridge. A lone deer (below) stands silhouetted amid fir trees while clouds form a fog blanket near a snow-crested mountain ridge at Olympic. The park's varied recreational fare includes a horseback climb (below left) through mountain highlands at Hayden Pass.

145

PETRIFIED FOREST

LOCATION: East-Central Arizona
SIZE: 94,189 acres
ESTABLISHED: 1962

Fossilized contours of an era claimed by the mists of time, and a vast horizon of alternately mingling, emerging reds, blue, browns and yellows—this is the Petrified Forest and Painted Desert combine of east-central Arizona. The "forest" of stone tree logs and trunks, coupled with the sweep of the desert's rainbow-like proscenium, constitutes a national park paradise which can be motored over, using the 34 miles of roads.

The stone forest emerges from a prehistoric period called the Triassic, over 180 million years ago, when pine-like trees grew beside streams which flowed through a seaside desert, similar to the present-day deserts of northern Chile. As best we know, the trees died of the same natural causes — fire, insects and old age — that decimate forests today. Some of the trees found in the park show signs of having been carried long distances by the early streams; others appear to have been buried where they grew.

Then the wondrous process of petrification took place along with patient sculpturing by nature. After the trees fell, they were buried by stream-carried mud and silt containing volcanic ash. In successive ages mile-thick deposits of similar material accumulated above the logs, mountain building lifted the logs far above sea level, and, comparatively recently, the logs and multicolored layers of the Painted Desert were exposed by erosion. During the time the trees were buried silica laden waters percolated into the air and pore spaces of the logs, filling these openings with multicolored quartz. Also during this period, earth tremors broke some of the logs into sections; others were fractured as erosion wore away the supporting earth.

The waters of the earth, which cyclically claim many of man's civilizations and landmarks, will, according to science, ultimately siphon away the color-charged clays, through erosion. Thus, we know that the Painted Desert will inevitably be sluiced away, as tons of silt, into the Gulf of California. Nevertheless, both the petrified logs and the wild, mixed colors of desert murals will be seen for many generations. Actually, only a part of the Petrified Forest is currently exposed. There are many other petrified logs scattered along substrata of the earth to a depth of about 300 feet.

In addition to the natural wonders preserved within the park, there exist about 300 archeological sites, spanning the period from about 300 A.D. to 1400 A.D. The pueblo (or cliff-dwelling) and other Indian cultures left in this area clear marks of their passage through time.

The unique wonder of the Painted Desert, especially for the tourist, is the titillating kaleidoscopic effect of changing colors. After rainfall, and following the shift of cloud shadows, the most stunning and varied suddenness of color combinations takes place.

Although visitors are not always conscious of the elevation of the park, it nonetheless ranges in height from 5,300 to 6,200 feet. The entire area receives less than ten inches of moisture annually and thus only hardy varieties of flowers add their smaller combina-

Brilliantly colored, the petrified logs receive their mottled patterns from oxides of iron and manganese.

tions of color to the phenomena above them.

The emphasis is upon delicate beauty with the blossoming of the yucca, mariposa-lily and cactus in the spring and the aster, painted-cup, or "paintbrush," the rabbitbrush and sunflower in bloom during the summer.

Birds, mammals, reptiles survive adequately in this barren museum of marvels. The jackrabbit, cottontail, squirrel and coyote are seen here as in other desertlands. The bobcat, porcupine and pronghorn antelope are more elusive, but omnipresent. Bird watchers know the diverse haunts of horned lark, house finch, rock wren, phoebe and sparrow in these wastes. And in this happy habitat of aridity are nearly three dozen species of snakes and lizards, including the prairie rattlesnake.

In the 1880's serious threats to the petrified wood through commercial exploitation and sheer vandalism aroused strong public protest and adroit Government action. At one point, logs were being blasted open for the amethyst crystals to be found within. Finally, on December 8, 1906, President Theodore Roosevelt created Petrified Forest National Monument by proclamation. In 1962 the area officially became Petrified Forest National Park, under the executive direction of the late President John F. Kennedy.

The park, in our own lives, and those of many future generations, exists, and will exist, for the interest and edification of the poet and beauty-lover in each of us, rather than for careless exploitation.

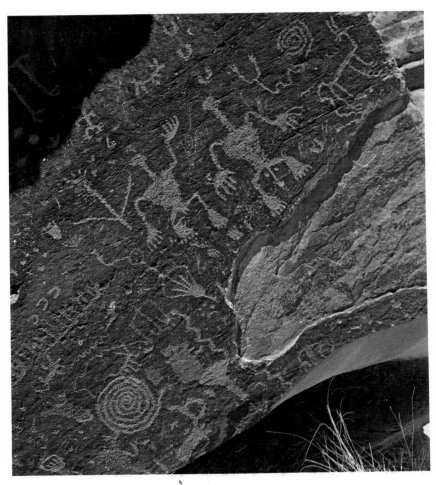

Painted Desert badlands (left) are typical of badland erosion. In places a hard covering of sandstone or lava have protected the soft layers beneath from torrential summer rains to form abrupt mesas and buttes. The Painted Cliffs (top) were formed by layers of an altered volcanic ash interlayered with minute amounts of iron oxide making layers of red, blue, brown and yellow. Newspaper Rock (bottom) is a series of petroglyphs believed to depict the events in the lives of Indians there long ago.

A young man tries his luck in peaceful Travertine Creek, fed by two fresh-water springs that have a combined water flow of five million gallons daily.

PLATT

LOCATION: Southern Oklahoma
SIZE: 912 acres
ESTABLISHED: 1906

Peaceful Valley of Rippling Waters, the Indians called Platt National Park. The Choctaws and Chickasaws treasured its quiet groves, bubbling mineral springs astride the confluence of the western plains and the wooded hills of the east.

Platt, our smallest national park, exists because the resident Indians were rigid in conservation and generous toward their fellow Americans. They gave over their Peaceful Valley, in 1902, to the United States on condition that it be preserved for the benefit of all the people.

In 1906 this preserve which now contains 912 acres became a national park, named for Senator Orville Platt of Connecticut, who had been prominent in Indian affairs.

There are some 30 mineral and fresh water springs in the park, seeping up through three major stratas of rock. The lower, or Simpson, group of rock provides the mineral salts for the bromide and sulphur springs with their varied solutions. At the eastern end of the park fresh water courses from Buffalo and Antelope Springs, named because herds of these animals came from the surrounding prairies to drink. Today the park is a preserve for a small herd of bison.

Prairie and woodland flowers abound in the flats and glades with a proliferation of redbud trees frequently dotting this richly endowed acreage of singing waters. These surroundings provide a home for various small mammals such as raccoon and armadillo.

Platt's gift lies in the identity of understanding between Indian intuition and this brief phrase of Henry David Thoreau: "In wildness is the preservation of the world."

Stonework around Buffalo Springs (above) was constructed by the Civilian Conservation Corps during the 1930's. An aerial view (below) of Platt National Park shows its winding streams and gentle foliage.

ROCKY MOUNTAIN

LOCATION: Northern Colorado
SIZE: 262,324 acres
ESTABLISHED: 1915

High over the mile-high city of Denver, 50 miles to the northwest, is the "roof of America." The 400 or more square miles of craggy heights which we know as Rocky Mountain National Park, in the Rocky Mountains, contains 107 named peaks over 11,000 feet in skyward reach.

What has been aptly called an alpine tundra is predominantly a terrain of few trees. Beyond the treeline ranges one third of the park area, with rolling, grassy slopes softening the panoramic onslaught of granite cliffs and spires.

In the two brief months of the highland summer the park is a land of enchantment, the atmosphere heady with the fragrance of tiny alpine wildflowers. In other seasons it is often bleak and desolate, windswept, with gales of arctic intensity swirling the snows into multiple hollows and crevices amid great peaks.

Far to the east, breathtakingly beautiful as seen from the uplands, the leveling edges of the Great Plains give one a literal sense of the immensity and variety of our continent. To the north, south and west, the skyline is broken by the serrated crests of other mountain ranges.

This is obviously the prime attraction for visitors: the view, as it were, from the top of our land. Unparalleled in its accessibility, because of the Trail Ridge Road, which winds through these uplands, tourists find themselves positioned, without need for the skill and strain of mountain climbing, at an elevation of 12,183 feet.

Historically, a route roughly following the Trail Ridge Road was used by the Utes and Arapahoes in crossing the Continental Divide. It was called Taieonbaa, the "Child's Trail," because it was so steep in places that children had to dismount from their horses and walk. Archeological research reveals that the Ute-Arapahoe Trail may have been in use for the past 8,000 years.

Unlike many of the Western national parks, there is little historical evidence that the area was extensively used by either Indians or whites in the exploration and winning of the West. Hunting parties from the tribes on either side of the Divide visited the area in summer on hunting trips. Berry-picking and just plain recreation were not unknown in these calming haunts. Trappers assessed the fur-bearing potential of the region — these, the informal explorers, must have been familiar with Longs Peak, awesomely viewed from the plains below. Two more formal parties, Lt. Zebulon Pike in 1806, and Major Stephen H. Long in 1820 — for whom the peak was named—charted the uncharted for future generations.

Hallett Peak in the Bear Lake area is one of 107 named peaks over 11,000 feet above sea level in the park.

In 1859 Joel Estes discovered the valley which was to bear his name. He moved his family to the "gorgeous gorge" and thus initiated further settlement of the town and valley now familiar as Estes Park.

The tremendous potential of the expanse of glaciated landscapes, as a national park, was grasped and articulated by surveyor and conservationist Enos Mills. At the tender age of 16 he had built a home in the Longs Peak valley in 1886. In 1891 he had filled his spirit enduringly working with a survey party in the Yellowstone. With a ferocity born of dedication to, and belief in conservation, he fought unceasingly for the ultimate establishment of Rocky Mountain National Park in 1915. Mills died in 1922, but some of his statements seem to have a touch of the immortality of the Rockies he loved and fought for: "Room — glorious room," he wrote, "room in which to find ourselves."

Today, about two million visitors annually enjoy the rugged and untrammeled beauty of the area. Meadows resplendent with wildflowers; forests of pine, spruce and fir; a variety of wild creatures in their natural habitat: American elk (wapiti), mule deer, black bear, coyote, cougar, can be glimpsed throughout lower and higher ranges of the park.

The solemn and symbolic bighorn, largest of American wild sheep, can be sighted — sandy-brown in summer, grayish-brown in winter — at Sheep Lake and on lonely promontories near Milner Pass in the northwest section of the park. The methodical beaver, lord of his dams, can be observed at several locations, including Horseshoe Park or Moraine Park, near the visitor center. In immaculate, pebble-bottomed streams, astringent with shallow, crystalline waters, stingingly frigid, fish trend toward anglers awaiting them in the lower levels. Trout is the resident of Rocky Mountain waters: brook, rainbow, cutthroat, with the latter native to the area. One of the principal lakes is Bear Lake in the south-central section.

Winter programs, the ski run and the ski lodge, are active around Hidden Valley, eight miles west of park headquarters. But springtime is the season of the Rockies, the season of bright wildflowers on the sunny slopes; and the meadows are a painter's heaven. Snow flurries with the sun's decline but does not endure before the heavy glare of the noonday sun. Summer in the park's tundra region doesn't really begin until July, but it is always summer in the spirit when the peace of the mountain grandeur descends upon those who seek its benisons.

154

From the Trail Ridge Road, the visitor can see from his car such sights as the Mummy Range (above). The road is often above the timberline (overleaf) where one can stop to view unusual rock formations.

With myriad lakes in rustic settings (above), one of the recreational offerings of Rocky Mountain is fishing. Fish in the park include cutthroat, brook, brown and rainbow trout. Rocky Mountain is the home of the bighorn sheep (above right), the wild sheep of the mountains. Known for speed, agility and endurance, this sheep, with massive, tightly curled horns, lives in mountains high above the timberline.

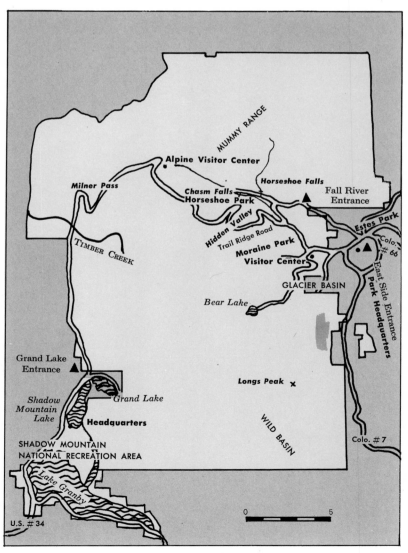

ROCKY MOUNTAIN NATIONAL PARK

Old in appearance, the Sierras in Sequoia are geologically young. Autumn colors cottonwoods below Mt. Langely (above), 14,042 feet high. On horse, a rider (right) enjoys Evolution Valley in Kings Canyon.

SEQUOIA

LOCATION: Southeast-Central California
SIZE: 386,863 acres
ESTABLISHED: 1890

and
KINGS
CANYON

LOCATION: Southeast-Central California
SIZE: 460,331 acres
ESTABLISHED: 1940

The tree is king here, peering down over a majestic domain of gray granite mountains, deep forests and valleys making a harsh but welcoming slash in the landscape. It stands, holding silent court over a seemingly untouched panorama, beginning beyond one horizon and going past the other.

This tree is the largest living thing in the world — rivaling the age of any tree or other plant known — the sequoia, gently elbowing aside white firs and sugar pines, its cinnamon-red bark and pointed needles quite unchanged from the time when frightening creatures rumbled the earth with their ponderous tread.

One can count nearly 4,000 years since some of them were born, and science believes none has died simply because of old age. They usually find their life-giving roots exposed by slow erosion, perhaps nature's way to return organic material to the soil. Then they topple and die with a crash, to lie fallen beside other warriors fighting the long battle against time in Sequoia and Kings Canyon National Parks.

There are more than 1,300 square miles in the two parks, starting at the foothills of the San Joaquin Valley and reaching toward the crest of the High Sierra. It is some 6,000 feet above sea level here, and the altitude makes the giant sequoias seem all the more regal. Perhaps at first, the height leaves one breathless, then suddenly the vista generates a catch in the lungs, for nowhere else does such a view exist.

Save for the efforts of a few, these mighty trees might have disappeared to the logger. The basis of the two parks gained Federal protection in 1890 so that they could be preserved. The culmination of this protection came in 1940 with the establishment of Kings Canyon National Park.

Hale Tharp was the first recorded visitor, a brawny, tanned cattleman seeking grazing land. He went up the Kaweah Valley near what is now Moro Rock, and listened to an Indian friend tell of the great mountain meadows lying beyond. Heartened, for cattle were his livelihood, Tharp followed the patrol of Indians to the meadows carpeted with deep, nutritional grass. There, in 1858, he beheld the Giant Forest's sequoias, and set up a temporary home in a fallen tree hollowed by fire.

Then, in 1862, Joseph Thomas discovered the General Grant Grove (now located in Kings Canyon Park) where several of the parks' outstanding trees reign. It took little time for their descriptions, and those of others, to create a national stir to preserve this virgin land.

Today, it all has changed. The parks are not what they were a century ago, nor are the trees the same. Although most of the changes are too small to measure, the valleys *are* a bit deeper because of erosion, the mountains a shade lower because of the torture of the elements, and some trees taller because the protective ring of the Government has given them life. If anything, Sequoia and Kings Canyon have grown more graceful, bearing their years with dignity.

The nucleus of a visit here is the General Sherman Tree, largest of all living things on earth, towering more than 272 feet above the ground and measuring more than 35 feet across the base. Because it is hard to imagine such a tree, perhaps this helps: the trunk alone weighs approximately 1,450 tons and has 50,010 cubic feet of wood, enough to build about 40 homes. The General Grant is only five feet shorter and contains only a bit less wood.

These giants of the forest live in harmony with their smaller and shorter-lived brethren. The gigantic sugar pines and firs wrest life from the soil, and even without the sequoias their existence would be a pleasing sight. They are youngsters, however, for the General Sherman is believed to be more than 3,500 years old, a fertile tree when Christ was born and existing when the great pyramids of ancient Egypt were being built. It is a living link with history; no, more than history, the evolution of our planet. Only one existing thing has been proved older, the bristlecone pine. And the young sequoias may be living after our civilization has become history.

Smaller than the sequoias, but with much value of their own, are the flora and fauna of the two parks. The floor of the forest is covered with dogwood, colorful lupine and the red-flowered snow plant. Meadows are filled with wildflowers, Sierra shooting stars in June, Queen Anne's lace and Senecio later. Bear and mule deer roam at will.

This is a rugged land, existing almost as a separate entity from the rest of the West. Beyond the Giant Forest, named by that great, Scots-born naturalist, John Muir, is the Sierra Nevada's high country, a vast, tilted block on the earth where snow-capped peaks — crowned by Mount Whitney, the highest mountain in the United States outside of Alaska —

The biggest and among the oldest of living things is the sequoia tree, sequoia gigantea.

rise to more than 14,000 feet to cast giant shadows on glacial valleys and ice-formed lake basins. This landscape is relatively untouched, existing as it is by Federal decree.

Here the bighorn sheep forages and the wolverine hunts among the alpine solitude, nuzzling through the luxuriant growth of a short summer, growing fat before the chill winds blow away the fragrance of delicate flowers and turn their vivid shades to dull brown, their colors not to return until spring.

Great canyons are incised upon the landscape, among the deepest to be found in the United States. Gorges along the middle and south forks of the Kings River are more than a mile deep, their steep sides forming a canyon between the great peaks and the roaring waters tumbling over time-polished stones below.

Here there are valleys, miles long and a half-mile wide, created when small streams grew larger and carried infinitesimal bits of stone with their downhill fury, then finally hewn to shape by vast fields of ice jamming their depths. The valleys bear silent testament to their past; glacial moraines telling of when nature's strength rubbed, scoured and finally gouged its way through granite, forming the canyon walls we see today.

Some of these valleys are covered with forests of ponderosa pine, incense-cedar and white fir, towering above blue lupine waving in the summer breeze. Deer, bear and bobcats graze and hunt among the trees. Birds flutter against wind gusts, then swoop earthward to grasp an insect in their beaks and retreat to the forest a few wing flaps beyond to enjoy their meal and perhaps sing of triumph.

High above—nearly two miles on top of the level of the sea—is a mountain wilderness dotted with glacial lakes mirroring the sun and its spectacular surroundings.

Magnificent, even in winter when snow festoons the giant sequoias and fills the dips and small valleys, there is no word that does justice to the parks and their environs.

The region so moved John Muir that he wrote, "No doubt these trees would make good lumber after passing through a saw mill, as George Washington after passing through the hands of a French chef would have made good food."

The sequoias, thankfully, are living, for their peculiar makeup gives them an odds-on chance against every natural enemy — except perhaps man.

While living in a cabin built in a single, fallen sequoia tree (left), Hale D. Tharp, the first white man to see the Giant Forest, used the area as a summer range for 30 years. The mule deer (above) finds a natural habitat at Sequoia with its forests, rocky uplands and brushy areas. Although the General Grant Tree (right) is the second largest of all sequoias, it is still 100 feet higher than Niagara Falls. This tree now serves as a shrine to America's war dead.

Nestled among decaying litter of pine and fir needles is the snow plant, a bright saprophyte.

Giants in the fog, the sequoias, have lived 40 centuries, protected by two-foot thick bark.

The flowering deer brush, or New Jersey tea, is a brilliant foreground to glacier-polished peaks of the Sierra Nevada. Favoring dry woodlands and high areas, it is a good winter food for grazing stock.

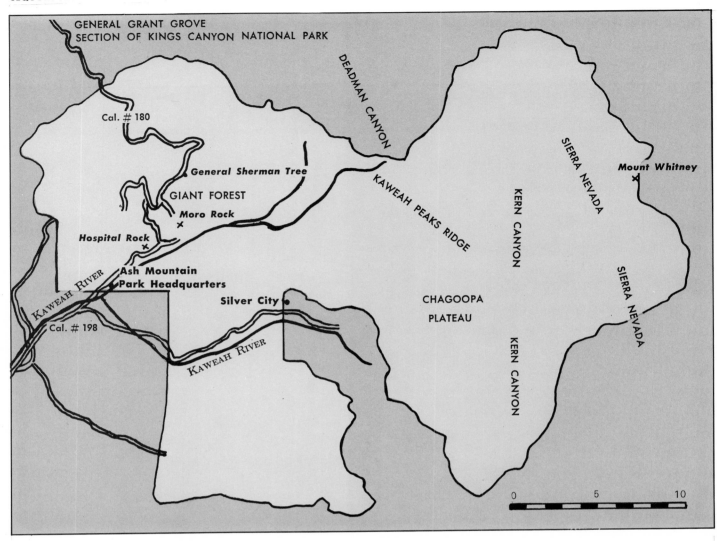

GENERAL GRANT GROVE
SECTION OF KINGS CANYON NATIONAL PARK

DEADMAN CANYON

Cal. # 180

General Sherman Tree

GIANT FOREST

Moro Rock

Hospital Rock

Ash Mountain
Park Headquarters

KAWEAH RIVER

Cal. # 198

Silver City

KAWEAH RIVER

KAWEAH PEAKS RIDGE

KERN CANYON

SIERRA NEVADA

Mount Whitney

CHAGOOPA
PLATEAU

KERN CANYON

SIERRA NEVADA

0   5   10

*K*earsarge Pass (right), at Kings Canyon, is over 11,500 feet above sea level. From there, mountain climbers can see rugged pinnacles of the same name. Tunnel Rock (above right), a man-made phenomena on the General's Highway, a half-mile from Sequoia's Ash Mountain Entrance Station, requires a by-pass road for many because of low clearance. Sparseness of trees at Pinchot Pass (far right), at over 12,000 feet, testifies that the pass is near the timberline.

The frequent bluish haze (above), for which Blue Ridge Parkway was named, is evident at Craggy Gardens near Asheville. Symbol of days past is the Brinegar Cabin (right) where historic looms are still used.

SHENANDOAH

LOCATION: Northwestern Virginia
SIZE: 193,539 acres
ESTABLISHED: 1935

and

BLUE RIDGE PARKWAY

LOCATION: Virginia and North Carolina
LENGTH: 659 miles
ESTABLISHED: 1936

This is a humble place where beauty is quiet and does not shout, where there is a tranquillity, a charm of blushing shyness that only gradually captures the visitor's awareness. But once its cup of gentle refreshment is drunk, one will find his pleasure and more.

This is Shenandoah, cradled against the breast of gentle mountains grown mellow with the age of the eastern half of our continent, spread in a generous north-south sweep down northwestern Virginia, encompassing great but not unconquerable mountains and brooks running in a grandfatherly way through the coolness of stately trees.

Yet, compared with other national parks, Shenandoah seems a lesser light until first the geological history is realized; finally its subtlety shines and one realizes there are few places left that can match its serenity. "Oh, Shenandoah, I Love Your Daughter," pleads the American folk song, and one wonders if its composer refers to the daughter of an Indian chief or the land named for the sachem. It is moot, for Shenandoah whispers of love, love of the land and its creatures.

This scene of green coolness and a long mountain range like a vein of blue is a great gift, for within a day's drive, over half of the nation's population can escape the tedium and anxieties of urban existence and sink into its quiet pleasure.

The Blue Ridge Mountains were first seen by Captain John Smith, and later by Alexander Spotswood, the Colonial governor of Virginia who crossed near what is now Swift Run Gap. George Freeman Pollock visited the Blue Ridge in 1886, and inspired by its beauty, spent a lifetime building a resort on Stony Man Mountain to let others succumb to the region's charm.

Pollock and friends proposed Shenandoah to a national committee, formed in 1925 to seek suitable park sites in the East. It was not an easy time for them; they struggled most of a night answering the committee's questionnaire, finishing it only a scant few hours ahead of the deadline.

Harry Flood Byrd, Sr., then governor of Virginia, supported their proposal and appointed his commissioner of conservation and development to oversee the purchase of lands for Shenandoah. The state legislature appropriated a million dollars, a vast sum in that time of hard cash, to help the park along. Added to it was a $1¼ million in the pennies, nickels and dimes of Virginians and others.

It was not until the eve of the Fourth of July, 1936, that Shenandoah National Park was a reality. President Franklin Delano Roosevelt dedicated it in ceremonies at Big Meadows, for the "recreation and re-creation which we shall find here."

*Re-*creation. It is two things spelled one way; only the pronunciation is different. For many who see Shenandoah, the accent is on the first syllable, for they are *re-*created here. They usually come by the Skyline Drive, a winding, 105-mile road threading across the crest of the Blue Ridge, offering 75 parking overlooks of the valleys and mountain slopes. Often they stop to leave the pavement and walk some of the 200 miles of foot trails. The hardy few who traverse the entire Appalachian Trail walk through Shenandoah, more than 90 miles of it.

Walking is the best way to enjoy the subtle pleasures of the park, such as seeing water shift its course to the other side of a rock, or feeling beneath one's feet the crunch of the brown, needle-strewn floor of the forest. A few yards beyond may be a handful of gnarled apple trees, unpruned for generations, surrounding a small clearing being rapidly overgrown with trees. Look closely, for here was the cabin of an early settler, one of the fur-capped frontiersmen who crossed these mountains on their way west. Some continued on, some remained. These old mountains were not really much of a natural barrier, but one so attractive many stayed, making it their home.

Hikers often climb Old Rag Mountain, starting near Nethers, Virginia, to complete the ascent and descent of eight miles in a day. There are shelters nearby. Others clop slowly along on horseback on the miles of bridle paths lacing the park.

The Shenandoah Valley was recognized as the Confederacy's "bread basket" and the back door to the nation's capital during the Civil War. General Stonewall Jackson brought troops within the park's boundaries during the struggle, and in Browns Gap there are earthworks believed to have been built by Confederate forces when they occupied the pass.

This is an old part of our land; more than a billion years in creation. Craggy peaks were smoothed by time into the gentle slopes of today, often wearing a mantle of the blue haze which gave the famous Blue Ridge its name.

The four seasons are each brilliant, painting new colors on the landscape from a palette of pastels with a handful of vivid shades. The dogwood and redbud come early in the spring as leaves from the 80-odd species of trees begin to unfold in the new-found warmth. Nearly seven-eighths of the park is forested, and in deep shaded glades the winter snows disappear slowly. Finally the sun brushes away the last patches of white, the water seeping into the ground to give life to plant and animal alike, often appearing as a cool spring a mile away or cascading down a rill.

Then the azaleas and locust come into bloom, followed by the pink and white mountain laurel. In patches of deep shade live the Dutchman's Breeches, a delicate, odd-appearing wildflower sharing the rich, moist soil with beard tongue and red blossoms of the cardinal-flower. Pushing its way through the carpet of black leaves here and there is the snowy trillium, a cousin of the turk's-cap lily covering low, grassy meadows.

In fall, as summer gives way to a new season, so that living things might sleep and regain their strength for a new spring, so that the mountain laurel will bloom again—come the colors, the wild reds, oranges, yellows and browns.

The Blue Ridge Parkway, separately administered but actually an extension of Shenandoah and Great Smokies National Parks, winds slowly from its lowest elevation crossing the James River in Virginia upward to its highest point of more than 6,000 feet in elevation in the Balsams south of Asheville, North Carolina. From it one can see the rolling hills of the Virginia Piedmont, across the fertile fields of the Great Valley, to the Alleghenies and then onward to the Black Mountains and the Great Smokies. Adjacent to the parkway are three national forests — the George Washington, the Jefferson and the Pisgah, which contains the first large tract of managed forest in this country.

In North Carolina's Black Mountains, Mt. Mitchell, 6,684 feet above sea level, is the highest peak in the eastern United States. Like other summits in the Blacks and the high Balsams, it is covered with spruce and fir, the two species of evergreens common to the wilds of Canada. Deer, bear, squirrels and one of the two herds of elk east of the Rockies roam up and down the mountainsides.

The parkway area is also rich in the folk history of the late 1700's: Log cabins and gristmills are preserved; Daniel Boone's Wilderness Road crosses the parkway in North Carolina.

Pleasures on a human scale are abundant in Shenandoah or along the Blue Ridge Parkway.

With much of Shenandoah forested, the 75 parking overlooks give excellent panoramas of the scenic hillsides.

As the Blue Ridge Parkway extends 469 miles through the Southern Appalachian Mountains, it tells the story of the original settlers, independent mountain people, through their homesteads and settlements.

Autumn is beautiful at Shenandoah and the Blue Ridge Parkway for then the trees catch fire with color.

A bird of the forests, the wild turkey finds a good life in the thickly wooded mountains of Shenandoah.

Mabry Mill was built in the late 1700's when Blue Ridge marked the edge of the western frontier. In use until 1936, it is preserved today with several other structures as evidence of a pioneer past.

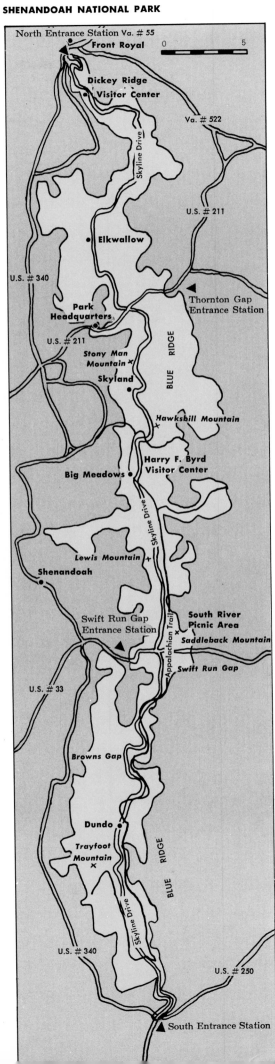

SHENANDOAH NATIONAL PARK

North Entrance Station Va. # 55

Front Royal

Dickey Ridge
Visitor Center

Va. # 522

Skyline Drive

U.S. # 211

Elkwallow

U.S. # 340

Thornton Gap
Entrance Station

Park
Headquarters

BLUE RIDGE

U.S. # 211

Stony Man
Mountain ×

Skyland

Hawksbill Mountain ×

Harry F. Byrd
Visitor Center

Big Meadows

Skyline Drive

Lewis Mountain +

Shenandoah

South River
Picnic Area

Swift Run Gap
Entrance Station

Saddleback Mountain ×

Appalachian Trail

Swift Run Gap

U.S. # 33

Browns Gap

Dundo

Trayfoot
Mountain ×

BLUE RIDGE

Skyline Drive

U.S. # 340

U.S. # 250

South Entrance Station

VIRGIN ISLANDS

LOCATION: Virgin Islands (St. John Island)
SIZE: 15,150 acres
ESTABLISHED: 1956

The essence of the Caribbean's soft, luxuriant, provocative moods is nowhere better captured than at Trunk Bay of Virgin Islands National Park. The green waters are rich with multihued varieties of colorful coral, sponges and exotic tropical fish. The shimmering white beaches are fringed with palms. Off shore stands an occasional islet. Above, a royal blue sky. Inland, the dominant terrain is composed of rugged tropical forests and Bordeaux Mountain, 1,277 feet high.

The park constitutes two-thirds of the Island of St. John, which is nine miles in length. The islands form a geological unit with Puerto Rico and the Greater Antilles, being of volcanic origin. St. John Island is a typical offspring of subsurface volcanic eruptions, dating back millions of years. Steep mountains, deep valleys, gleaming white beaches and extensive coral reefs growing on an underwater shelf of rock are characteristic of this unique national preserve. These are the islands that were discovered by Christopher Columbus on his second voyage, in 1493. He named them in honor of St. Ursula and her 11,000 virgins.

Prior to the incursions of the Europeans, villages of the peaceful Arawak Indians dotted the shores of St. John. Rock carvings called petroglyphs can still be seen here, suggestive of ancient shrines. Prepared to give Columbus and his succeeding voyagers a warm reception, however, were the fierce Caribs who had come from South America a century earlier and were encroaching steadily on Arawak lands.

After 1493, Dutch, English, Spanish, French and Danish explorers came to the Virgin Islands. The Danes, who left a more permanent mark, did not establish themselves on St. John until 1717. Arable land was cultivated for sugar and cotton crops and the plantations were manned by slaves imported from Africa. The sugar trade flourished until slavery was abolished in 1848, an economic and social blow to a powerful planter aristocracy. The ex-slaves turned to fishing, charcoalmaking, cattle raising, but they and their picturesque descendants remained generally poor. Tourism is currently the primary industry of the islands.

Following the demise of the plantations in the mid-1800's, tropical forests inexorably returned substantial areas of the island to its "natural habitat." Thus, the island resembles the one which Columbus first looked upon, plus the exotic flowers, trees and shrubs introduced by the settlers. Amid tropical luxuriance, however, the ruins of Danish sugar mills can still be seen.

Strategically commanding approaches to the Caribbean and Atlantic as they do, the islands were of great interest to the security of the United States. Thus, intensive negotiations, at first unsuccessful, took place

Dating from the mid-1700's, the Annaberg estate ruins emerge from a green promontory above Leinster Bay.

between the American Government and Denmark, beginning in 1867. The islands were finally purchased in 1917 for $25 million, administered earlier by the U.S. Navy, and later by a resident Governor.

The relatively moist interior highlands of St. John, including steep-walled valleys, are dominated by a jungle forest of evergreen hardwoods. Drier slopes contain broad-leaved trees. Mangroves, turpentines, maho, cinnamon-bay kapok and soursop are the characteristic trees. Flowering shrubs and trees bloom in season, with a charm for the tourists increased by the knowledge that hibiscus, flamboyant, frangipani, bougainvillea, are expensive commercial items back in the floral hothouses of the States.

About 100 species of birds abound in the islands with land birds more dominant. Herons, egrets, pelicans, gulls, frigate birds and terns can, however, be spotted along the shores. The pearly-eyed thrasher, smooth-billed ani, the mocking and humming birds are discernible in the forests and hills.

Six forms of bats are the only native mammals, although several species have been introduced, the best known being the mongoose. There are also toads, lizards, turtles, snakes and the hermit crab, which, oddly, lives in discarded top shells. Insects are minimal with the exception of the mosquito and pesky sand fly which multiply after rainy spells.

Snorkeling is a major activity in the park. Visitors have a chance to snorkel along the underwater trail at Trunk Bay, participate in a naturalist-led snorkel trip at Turtle or Cinnamon Bays or explore on their own in a number of other good snorkeling areas (Hawksnest, Leinster, Francis and Lameshur Bays). The water here is warm and clear. The commonly seen features of this marine world are antler, brain and star corals (that make up the reef's structure); gorgonians (sea fans, sea plumes and sea whips); sponges; and a great variety of colorful marine fishes.

The northeast trade winds temper the intense heat of the tropical sun, yielding pleasantly warm days and cool nights. The average annual temperature is 79 degrees with only about 6 degrees difference between the winter and summer seasons. The lowest temperature on record is 60 degrees, the highest, 96. It is readily apparent why winter is the busiest visitors' season.

St. John Island's beauty, spiced with coral reef, tropical forest and history, is a matchless part of the national heritage.

Caneel Bay (above), site of the park's most extensive guest facilities, is also an excellent area for sailing. Bayside cottages and beach units for visitors now stand where European plantation owners grew cotton and sugar cane in the 18th century. Expert gliders, ring-billed gulls (above right) fly gracefully near the multihued sea and lush green woodlands. Trunk Bay (right) features a self-guiding underwater trail through spectacular natural displays of coral and other marine life for experienced snorkel swimmers.

Jungle forests (left) dominate the interior highlands and ravines of the park, their rapid growth requiring constant clearing by machete-wielding trail workers. The sugar mill ruins at Annaberg (above), are among several stone reminders of St. John Island's history. Built by European settlers who established large plantations in the early 1700's, the structures became fortifications during a slave uprising in 1733.

WIND CAVE

LOCATION: Southwestern South Dakota
SIZE: 28,059 acres
ESTABLISHED: 1903

Wind Cave's 44 square miles above ground contain many bison, as well as deer, elk and other wildlife.

The wind blows east, the wind blows west, and from the other two points of the compass, also. But it doesn't usually blow up through the ground. Yet cowboy Tom Bingham, wandering through the southern Black Hills in 1881, felt the upward draft and stooped in puzzlement, touched with wonder. There he saw a ten-inch natural opening in the limestone rock of the hill — and what could he call it but Wind Cave.

Afterward, explorers got into the cave by digging entrances near the original "blow-hole." Within were the fairyland formations on walls and ceilings, resembling a honeycomb or "boxwork" structure that might have intrigued a Tom Sawyer and Huck Finn into dark and forbidding recesses.

One might first imagine that another aperture higher on the hill would be the air intake. But that is not the case. This strange phenomenon of a breathing hill is believed to be caused by changes in atmospheric pressure. The cave actually completes the cycle of breathing, as it were, by letting in the wind when the outside pressure rises, and by expelling air when the pressure drops.

The weird ornamentation of Wind Cave is unique among famed caverns in that it includes relatively few stalagmites and stalactites. The boxwork was created by a layer of limestone which was sculptured and form-frozen in varied periods of geological uplift and submergence. Then, moisture containing calcium carbonate, seeped through and evaporated, depositing the calcium carbonate, forming calcite in the cracks.

More recently the limestone between the fissures dissolved, leaving calcite fins, some lace-like, some broad enough to resemble the sides of boxes and thus called "boxwork." This variegated effulgence is additionally decorated with arresting displays of mineral colors in the form of tiny, sparkling crystals called "frostwork" and formations that look like yuletide arrangements of "popcorn."

The central attraction of Wind Cave National Park, the cavern, is rivaled in naturalistic lure by the wildlife sanctuary surrounding it. Over the park's 44 square miles of rolling woodlands and plains, graze herds of the historic bison, once slaughtered by callous white men from Pullman car and saddle alike. The bison, more popularly known as buffalo, is rich in legend. Staff of life for the Indians, and the shield against wind and storm in the hides of the red men's teepees, the bison later became a thoroughly American symbol in terms of the settlement of the wild West. Antelope, elk and deer, in herds, also graze among the lush rises and flatlands of the park.

Biologically speaking, east meets west in Wind Cave National Park, where ponderosa pine, typical of the Western mountains, grow on the same slopes with eastern bur oaks. And the animals graze on what is a prime example of mixed-grass prairie, a rich natural blending of medium tall and short grasses, with a sprinkling of wildflowers which lend dashes of color to the scene.

Here, in virginal splendor, is one of the last of the portions of the great Western plains. Here in South Dakota are wonders in number: the breathing cave; the historic, wild sea of grass, rippling in the wind; the mighty buffalo.

*P*ark ranger (left) viewing park's landscape. "Chandelier boxwork" in Temple Room (above) is fine example of the unique formation for which Wind Cave is known. Pasqueflower (top right) is South Dakota's state flower. Pronghorn (bottom right), one of the two sole living American kinds of antelope, makes its home in the park.

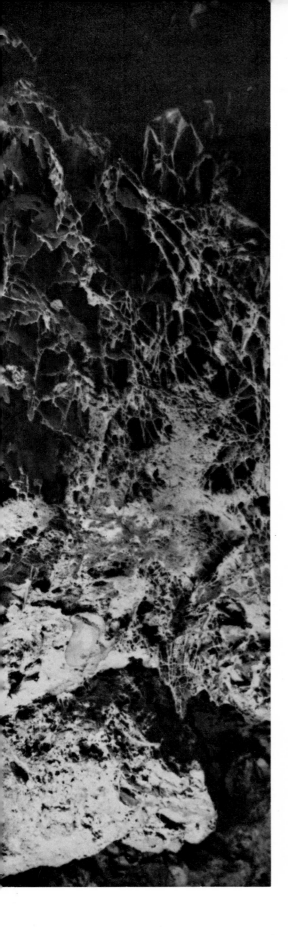

YELLOWSTONE

LOCATION: Northwestern Wyoming, Eastern Idaho and
Southern Montana

SIZE: 2,221,773 acres

ESTABLISHED: 1872

It is like the creation of the very devil himself: Angry forces of the underworld locked in combat beneath the earth with the sounds and visible fury of their struggle seeping through fissures to enthrall the curious above ground who come to see what the forces of fire and ice have spawned.

This is Yellowstone National Park in the northwest corner of Wyoming (and narrow strips of Idaho and Montana), where nearly all that nature has to offer has been concentrated in a spectacular display unmatched anywhere on earth. Boiling springs, steam vents, mudpots spewing mud and, as a climax, the great geysers hurtling tons of water hundreds of feet skyward — these dot the otherwise pastoral land to make a strangely beautiful if not sometimes forbidding world.

The park's strange landscape had its origin some 20 million years ago when Yellowstone, then a mountain-rimmed basin, became the seat of violent volcanism. Clouds of dust and ash filled the air. Settling shroud-like over the land, it buried entire forests. Fiery cascades of semi-molten rock rolled down the mountainsides, and great fissures belched forth enormous volumes of highly fluid lava. Some 600 cubic miles of this molten rock was spewed out onto the land. The mountain-rimmed basin filled; it was a basin no longer, and Yellowstone became a high plateau.

But a few scars remained, as did a handful of open wounds which could never quite heal because of the cancerous fury far beneath. The heat of these prehistoric volcanoes remains, much like a storage battery to provide power for the sights which greet the visitor today.

Old Faithful is aptly named, for it is prompt, appearing about once an hour, day and night, hurling 15,000 gallons of hot water in a single, magnificent unleashing of force. There are few other places in the world where such phenomena exist — New Zealand, Chile and Iceland.

Old Faithful has 200 cousins at Yellowstone, among them the Riverside, Grotto, Castle and Beehive geysers, all sustained in the same way. Cold water from the long winter's melted snows finds its way through the hard volcanic rock around the geysers. Thousands of feet below the surface it is heated by hot rocks and also by gases and natural steam escaping from still deeper molten rock. Soon the cool water begins to boil, building pressure as steam forms, forcing the water higher into the geyser column. Then as the pressure is relaxed, huge quantities of steam are formed within the underground chambers, forcing the column of water to the surface in a pulsating, continuous finger of dancing liquid, pirouetting on the surface for four or five minutes. Suddenly the mad ballet ends, the crown of vapor floats skyward and the water recedes as the energy of the steam dissipates. Then, it begins again in the mighty flexing of muscles which has become America's best-known natural wonder.

With this fire which has shaped the face of Yellowstone, there is also ice — the great glaciers which formed on the mountains to the north and east when the fires cooled and died, on the surface at least. These unyielding masses, some 1,000 and more feet thick, began to move downward, bringing with them the inorganic scrapings of the land over which they passed. Small valleys were deepened and widened,

Sunlight captures the power of steaming water as it erupts from Castle Geyser at Yellowstone National Park.

189

some mountains were sharpened and others ground level. The ice melted, leaving lakes which have long since disappeared.

The rest of Yellowstone is not quite so forbidding, but has a rugged loveliness all its own: A cliff of obsidian, or black volcanic glass, overlooks columns of lava rock; a steady flow of the hot springs is seen a few miles beyond Obsidian Cliff; fossil forests exist in silence not too far from craggy mountains caressed with the green of conifers; a multitude of wildlife roams fearlessly through great forests of pine; roaring waterfalls plummet into a yellow rock canyon, the sun forming a rainbow above its splashing waters.

The stories of the early travelers to Yellowstone, such as John Colter in 1807-1808, were looked upon with skepticism. But the tales continued, and finally in 1870 Yellowstone was officially "discovered." Two years later it became the nation's and the world's first national park.

Even after it became the first of the great park system, it was not a safe place for tourists. While some Indians possibly lived in fear of the geysers, the Bannocks, Shoshones, Blackfeet and Crows raided and murdered hunters, trappers and explorers. In 1877, the Nez Perce turned to violence, killing some visitors, then burned a ranch north of the park.

Yellowstone's noises of the 20th century are not those of war-painted red men, but those of winds brushing tree limbs, the rumble of water crashing to far-below canyons and the whisper of rain on the high plateau. It is the sound of deer and American elk (wapiti) browsing on the deep green carpet of meadows, the rattle of stones under the feet of the majestic bighorn sheep clambering up a steep wash, the frightened snort of the pronghorn antelope fleeing into the wind, the earth-shaking rumble of the great and shaggy buffalo racing red-eyed across a flat plain, the mournful cry of the coyote and the angry roar of the grizzly bear.

These creatures, one of the greatest concentrations of native American wildlife in the nation, roam about the park in impressive numbers, joining to drink in spring and fall at the pools where great flights of migrating waterfowl pause to rest. They each have found their environmental niche at Yellowstone, wading in the marshes, flitting from tree to tree or browsing on tender green shoots in the forests where there is a cool respite from the summer sun.

High above much of the park is Yellowstone Lake, a body of water stretching 20 miles in one direction, 14 in the other. Its mirror-like surface can be broken into giant whitecaps within minutes as storms blow in from the snow-capped Rockies beyond, or great bolts of lightning are discharged between the surface and the sky.

Travel this lake in a boat to its outlet where the Yellowstone River begins its course, a clear, swift-running stream knifing through green forests and past grassy meadows. Then the soft but persistent stream becomes more determined as it shoots out in a straight line to the base of the Upper Falls 109 feet below. A deep gorge holds it fast until the burgeoning water pours over the lip of the Lower Falls through a narrow notch, dropping more than 300 feet accompanied by a thunderous crash and gale of wind. It is here, where the river has cut over a thousand feet into the highly colored rocks, that the Grand Canyon of the Yellowstone begins. This, one of the most beautiful of canyons in the world, is best viewed from Artist's Point, Inspiration Point or Grandview.

The weather, like the park itself, has great contrasts. Winters are fierce and snow falls relentlessly to fill great earth cavities. Storms make cruel blows at the plateaus, bringing awesome amounts of snow and ice. It melts slowly, but fortunately it arrives each year, for without this ponderous volume of water the geysers would fail, the hot springs dwindle to a trickle then die and finally the two spectacular falls would become but a dribble and streams would dry, upsetting the ecological balance of all that lies to the south.

But fortunately, it seems nothing will change in Yellowstone for the forces of nature are not easily swayed. Here there is no man-made edifice or unnatural changes by machine. There is no skyscraper, except some of rock, or hole torn in the earth, except the slowly evolving depression caused by water and wind today and the volcanoes or glaciers of yesterday. There is peace and ultimate grandeur in Yellowstone, a legacy left by nature and administered for all the heirs of tomorrow.

The Absaroka Mountains extend for 175 miles into northwestern Wyoming including Yellowstone National Park.

Canoeists on Yellowstone Lake have a mighty backdrop with the Absaroka Mountains to the east.

A gnarled ponderosa pine looks on the Grand Canyon of the Yellowstone from the top of Mount Washburn.

Calcium carbonate deposits terrace colorfully at Mammoth Hot Springs forming a quasi-frozen waterfall.

The Lower Falls of Yellowstone River (above) changes 1,200 cubic feet of bottlegreen water into frothy white jets plunging 309 feet into the gorge below.

Old Faithful Geyser (below) erupts regularly every 65 minutes shooting 15,000 gallons of water 125-175 feet into the air. Eruptions last several minutes.

Early evening skies are reflected in the Firehole River as it meanders past the Midway Geyser Basin.

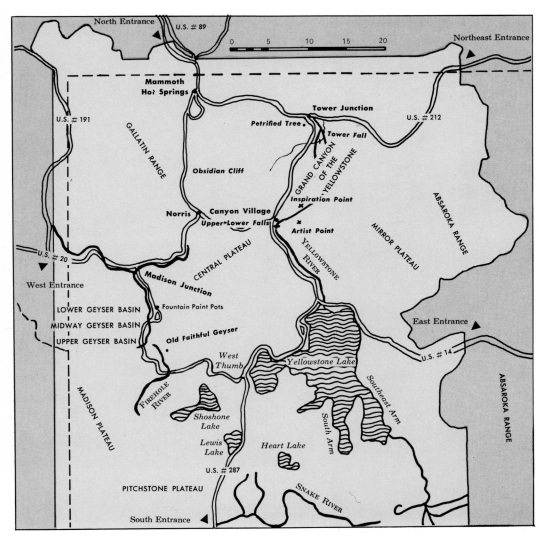

YELLOWSTONE NATIONAL PARK

The American elk (wapiti) is the largest deer in the United States. He makes a far-carrying bugle sound.

Trumpeter swan stay at Yellowstone all year because the water is heated from hot springs and geysers.

The thermal activity of the Norris Geyser Basin includes a variety of small geysers plus the violent and unpredictable Steamboat Geyser which has hurled steam and water as high as 300 feet into the air.

YOSEMITE

LOCATION: East-Central California
SIZE: 761,320 acres
ESTABLISHED: 1890

Long recognized for beauty and scenic resources, Yosemite has been protected for over 100 years. Known for variety — glaciated peaks and domes, high mountain falls, giant sequoias and subalpine meadows—Yosemite is the epitome of a national park. Rising 3,600 feet above Merced River in the Yosemite Valley is El Capitan, a granite monolith.

The dawn sun lies poised over Yosemite National Park, then the murmuring thunder of Bridalveil Creek seems to bring forth the hushed melody of the early morning wind blowing through spires of the groves of sequoias and evergreens as life stirs in this idyllic retreat in the High Sierra of California.

Whatever the season, winter of great snow or the pinnacle of summer, Yosemite lives on, its shape infinitely changing under the slow but persistent hand of nature.

Yosemite was born a hundred million years ago, but she carries her age with grace, growing more desirable with the millenniums. The Sierra Nevada gave birth to her, quaking with the pains of labor as the granite mass rose higher to the east, creating streams which drained into the Merced River.

The Merced grew in strength, not unlike a giant artery, flowing toward the San Joaquin Valley to cut a canyon 2,000 feet deep in the rolling upland surface. In Yosemite's puberty, the glaciers came, gouging the V-shaped canyon into a wider and deeper U-shaped trough.

Bridalveil was one of the creeks — Yosemite and Ribbon were others — which lost their lower extremities to the mighty glaciers, leaving the valleys hanging. These streams then plummeted into the valley. Then the glaciers melted, leaving hundreds of tons of water behind a moraine, or a natural dam of rock debris, forming a lake which in time became filled with silt, sand and rock to form the level valley floor we see today.

The wonders of Yosemite range from the awesome crash of water to canyons far below to the pastoral silence of flower-flocked meadowlands.

Congress saw its great beauty in 1864, and granted it to the State of California. In 1890 the national park was created around this Yosemite Grant. California ended its control of the grant in 1905, turning it back over to the Federal Government to form an enlarged national park. There are now nearly 1,200 square miles for all to enjoy, protected forever against the encroachment of man and his penchant for reshaping the face of nature.

But man has not just recently discovered Yosemite. The Ahwahneechee Indians lived here long before it was discovered by the white man. Their name for it, taken from the tribal description, was Ahwahnee, or "deep, grassy valley in the heart of the sky mountains."

A doe and her fawn nibble the grass in one of the four distinct life zones at Yosemite National Park.

Then, a little over a hundred years ago, the Mariposa Battalion, a band of miners, entered the valley, seeking retribution for Indian raids. Some of the miners, awed by the expansive beauty of the region, argued around a campfire, trying to name their surroundings. They finally agreed on "Yosemite," perhaps meaning "grizzly bear." It was a derivation of U-zu-ma-ti, the name of a sub-group of Chief Tenaya's tribe, who then inhabited the valley.

While the Mariposa Battalion's visit was the first recorded trip by white men, it is believed the Joseph Walker party touched on part of the park in their journey of 1833. Nonetheless, to the growing nation just beginning to discover itself in those few short years before the Civil War, Yosemite enthralled the young country.

Members of the battalion wrote enthusiastically of Yosemite, and four years later, in 1855, James M. Hutchings brought the first tourist party. This group would, a shade over a hundred years later, be only a millionth of Yosemite's annual visitors.

Hutchings, the publisher of *California Magazine*, wrote glowing articles extolling the natural virtues of

Yosemite, then where words failed, illustrated his pieces with sketches by Thomas Ayres. Hutchings' eloquent prose was reprinted by other publications, and soon Americans came to see for themselves. Californians, spirited by the great wonder which had been left in their midst, became concerned over Yosemite's future. In 1864, President Abraham Lincoln signed the Yosemite Grant, ceding it to California, to be held "inalienable for all time."

Thus, Yosemite became the first public park to be administered by a state government, and dictated the concept which has since served as the basis for the current National Park System.

It was fitting that this splendid region be such a first. There are hundreds of miles of trails leading from the valley through the coolness and fragrance of deep woods; across the sun-splashed meadows to high mountain lakes teeming with fish growing fat and ferocious in their chill depths.

But let us start at the valley, seven square miles of cragginess that becomes beautiful at once to the beholder. Mountainsides and cliffs overhang the canyon where the Merced River threads. A few miles

Upper and Lower Yosemite Falls (above) have a total drop of 2,425 feet. Tuolumne Meadows (below) is the largest subalpine meadow found in the High Sierra.

later, the roadway widens to a flower-flecked meadow, dominated by El Capitan, a flawless granite monolith rising more than 3,600 feet toward the sky. Nearly as imposing are the Cathedral Spires, Sentinel Rock and the Three Brothers named for the sons of Chief Tenaya whose domain this land once was.

Water shaped Yosemite, and still is slowly wearing away rock as it must, seeking the lower levels and carrying with it bits of stone and vegetable matter, endlessly creating. The Upper Yosemite Fall drops 1,430 feet, and the Lower a bit less than a fourth of that. Water cascades with a roar over the top of cliffs for a total drop of 2,425 feet from the crest of the Upper Fall to the base of the Lower.

Not all is the sound and fury of nature. There is solitude in Yosemite to be found in her stands of sequoias, one, the Grizzly Giant, believed to have been born from seed more than 3,000 years ago. This magnificent cousin of the redwood is 209 feet tall and is more than 34 feet in diameter across the base. Growing silently, contributing to its grandeur, are the park's incense-filled forests of pine and fir and cedar and oaks, providing habitat for band-tailed pigeons, pygmy owls, chipmunks and squirrels.

Deer and bear pause to feed here, then move on to the high country, a land of lakes and meadows, capped by high peaks casting great dark shadows on the rainbow of wildflowers below. Tuolumne Meadows at 8,600 feet is the largest subalpine meadow in the High Sierra. Though it can be best enjoyed on foot, there are auto roads leading to jewel-like Tenaya Lake and Tioga Pass, between granite bolders polished to a shine by the glaciers and past high domes of the same stone. Another road leads from the valley 30 miles to Glacier Point, giving a panoramic view of the High Sierra and the valley 3,300 feet below.

In spring, there is a flood of color—brilliant yellows and soft blues with the dark green of the conifers filling the eye with the splendor of an untouched land. In winter, the high country is forbidding when giant snows fill the land, only to melt into the trickle of mountain streams which become the raging torrent to start life anew in this land of 10,000 wonders.

John Muir, the great Scots-born naturalist, saw its contrasts: "the most songful streams in the world . . . the noblest forests . . . the loftiest granite domes . . . the deepest ice-sculptured canyons."

The Merced River drops over 900 feet when it reaches the 594-foot drop at Nevada Fall followed quickly by a 317-foot plunge at Vernal Fall. Seen from Glacier Point, Half Dome's bald face is to the left.

Bridalveil Fall drops between the Cathedral Rocks 620 feet, often swaying from frequent gusts of wind.

Half Dome (above), 8,852 feet high, rises majestically over Tenaya Creek. At the east end of Yosemite Valley, Mirror Lake (below) reflects the image of Mount Watkins.

Lembert Dome (left), in the Toulumne Meadows, unlike Half Dome, was polished by glacial action. Half Dome and others were formed by exfoliation, the cracking and expansion of rock layers which round off angular surfaces. The total immensity of Upper and Lower Yosemite Falls (right), seen in the background on page 203, is revealed by a close-up from a tree-lined road leading from Yosemite Village.

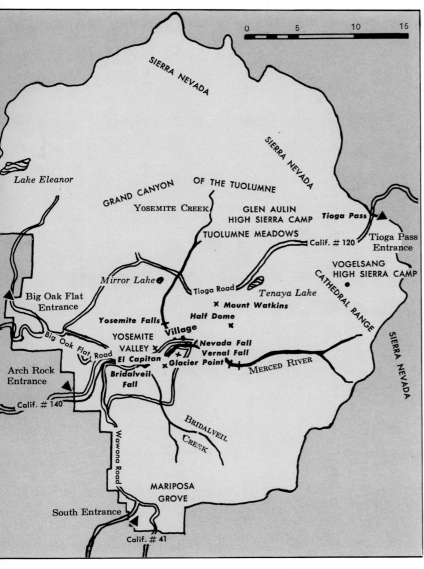

YOSEMITE NATIONAL PARK

"Canyonland in color." That is Zion National Park in Utah which Mormon pioneers, in 1858, called a place of "peace and comfort," articulating the grandeur of infinite being which its 135,256 acres overwhelmingly suggests.

Ranging across the plateau and canyon region of southwestern Utah, the park's sheer-wall formations in color are unique among the world's geological phenomena. Over 150 million years of natural processes formed all this beauty. Here, visitors can actually follow the path of the large three-toed dinosaur and discern his huge footprints in hard sandstone rock layers. His distant cousins in the form of reptiles and amphibians still abound, yet the only deadly survivor of ages past, there in the park, is that dramatic insurgent of pioneer life, the rattlesnake.

Thirteen million years ago, the area, long a bottom for surging and subsiding seas, was lifted thousands of miles through phenomena such as mile-high deposits of sediment. The erosion of this uplifted plateau formed the domes, peaks and canyons that now have become familiar.

The native inhabitants of this region, the peaceful Paiute Indians, first looked upon the white man during the Escalante-Dominguez explorations in 1776. Fifty years later, Jedediah Smith led a party of trappers and fur traders into previously inaccessible reaches near this region, prowling and plodding in quest of pelts from Great Salt Lake south though the valleys probably to the Virgin River.

The gallant and intrepid Captain John C. Fremont, in his 1843-1844 explorations of the great Southwest, garnered the geographic certainties of primeval wonder which were to excite the imagination and determination of dedicated Mormon pioneers in 1847. Within a decade the Mormons had settled around the Virgin River and named the region, appropriately, Zion, "the heavenly city of God."

Major John Wesley Powell explored the region in 1872 and named the canyon of the north fork of the Virgin River "Munkuntuweap" and the canyon of the east fork "Parunuweap," Indian designations influencing the earliest identity of the park as a national monument in 1909. But the prevailing Mormon

ZION

LOCATION: Southwestern Utah
SIZE: 147,035 acres
ESTABLISHED: 1919

Rising above the Virgin River is Angels Landing, a sandstone monolith which is representative of the name Zion, the heavenly city of God. A stiff climb on foot and horse trails provides an excellent view of Zion Canyon from this 1,500-foot perch.

influence and flavor wrought the change to Zion National Park, and also its expansions in 1937 and 1956.

Greenery tumbles richly about the banks of the Virgin, contrasting breathtakingly with the majestic red of Navajo sandstone precipices and the intense blue of the skies overhead. To the northwest can be seen Horse Ranch Mountain, 8,740 feet high, towering above all the great cliffs of the park.

East of the highway, driving north along the effervescent north fork of the Virgin River, the Watchman, 6,555 feet, glows like a vast reddish-brown jewel in the glints and starts of a remorseless sun. The driver-distracting panorama continues up Zion Canyon, a distance of eight miles, to the Temple of Sinawava. To the left, in succession, are the reverently named heights: the Towers of The Virgin, the Altar of Sacrifice, the Beehives, Sentinel Peak, the Three Patriarchs, Majestic Mountain and Angels Landing; to the right, East Temple, Mount Spry, the Twin Brothers, Mountain of the Sun, Red Arch Mountain and the Great White Throne.

Beyond the Great White Throne, river and road twist to the west at The Organ, behind which Angels Landing rises 1,500 feet above canyon bed. Cable Mountain is on the right, now. A 6,496 foot peak, it takes its name from a 2,136-foot cable, used by lumbermen in 1900 to transport lumber from the east rim into the canyon. To the west is Cathedral Mountain with Observation Point and The Pulpit, soaring to the right and left. At the Temple of Sinawava the road ends, yielding to a trail toward The Narrows. Here the canyon narrows to a 1,500 foot chasm only a few feet wide and with sheerness of cliff pressing the hiker closely on both sides.

Zion Canyon has well been called a threshold or point of departure. It is only a beginning, for trails lead out of the canyon onto the highland plateau and far into the back country where unviolated wilderness is supreme. Paramount, and especially unique to Zion and its far reaches, is the instant understanding of Henry Van Dyke's phrase: "A national park should be as sacred as a temple."

Trails lead to overlooks, too, such as the one atop Angels Landing or to Observation Point at the end of the East Rim Trail. Here, as almost everywhere in Zion is what Enos Mills called "glorious room—room in which to find ourselves, in which to think and hope, to dream and plan, to rest and resolve."

From here the view of Zion Canyon offers a

unique geologic insight into the whole Zion region. Far below lies the meandering Virgin River, tortuous in its windings around each bend of rock on its way to Lake Mead of the Colorado.

The Virgin River is responsible for the inch by inch, eternal and incessant carving of Zion Canyon. The river has never been much larger than it is today and this is a clue to the fact that the river and its tributaries are not a fisherman's paradise—although fishing is permitted in the park. Frequent flooding and shiftings of silt and sand are not kind to the survival of trout in the stream and its offshoots.

Animals indigenous to the mountains and arid areas survive in this region, and the cough of the cougar, the chilly plaint of the coyote can be heard on the land. Bobcats, foxes, weasels, squirrels and chipmunks are numerous. Here the golden eagle and hawk are king and princeling among the feather-bearers. The wiry species of road-runner, spurred towhee, Rocky Mountain nuthatch, are extremely deft in avoiding the two aforementioned "dive-bombers" of the peaks.

The piñon pine, gnarled juniper, deep-green forests of Douglas and white fir flourish. And the golden aspen of autumn flourishes when moisture and soil are plentiful. Here are found the magical night-flowers, the jimson weed (or thornapple), the white-evening primrose and the ferns and grasses rich along the river and trickling streams.

In winter only the higher trails are unnegotiable because of snow. The contrasts of red sandstone amid blinding sun glancing off snow drifts can be productive of bizarre loveliness to behold. And in spring the cascades plummet in foaming furies over the sheer faces of the cliffs.

Such is Zion, the bequest of forgotten, prehistoric seas. "A great reservoir," as Donald Culross Peattie once wrote, "of the serene order of nature."

Cycles of geology for 150 million years — slow uplifting, vast seas, violent earth upheavals, weather and erosion — are responsible for such fascinating formations at Zion as the Great White Throne (opposite) and the Three Patriarchs (below). Both rise as part of the walls of Zion Canyon and can be seen on trips of varying lengths on foot or horse trails.

GUADALUPE MOUNTAINS

LOCATION: Southwestern Texas
SIZE: 82,279 acres
AUTHORIZED: 1966

A spring flows through South McKittrick Canyon, providing moisture for the many plants and animals.

In the middle of the Chihuahuan desert of southwestern Texas is an "island in the sky." One-quarter of the Guadalupe Mountain Range dips across the New Mexico border here, only a few miles southwest of Carlsbad Caverns National Park. These uplands contain a startling diversity of flora and fauna in an unusual mountain-desert setting, and it is fitting that, in 1966, Congress designated them as the nation's thirty-third national park.

The most notable feature of the Guadalupes is Y-shaped McKittrick Canyon — a deep cut in the northeastern mountains which embraces a unique, balanced ecosystem. Here the vegetation ranges from desert scrub to forests of pine, fir and juniper.

A wide variety of birdlife coexists with coyotes, foxes and bobcats which prey on various rabbits and

rodents. Elk, mule deer and pronghorns drink from the self-replenishing streams and springs, and wild turkeys and quail dodge through the brush. A few blue-throated hummingbirds—a rare and endangered species—and spotted owls exist here, but there are also many varieties of birds common in distant sections of North America which are geographically isolated in this national park, including water ouzels, bandtailed pigeons and brown creepers. This area also once supported desert bighorns and wolves, but they among other species have been driven out, and black bears, mountain lions and golden eagles are now few in number. But McKittrick Canyon is still unsullied, for its high, precipitous walls and narrow canyon have fortunately discouraged "development" by man.

The park has many other fascinating features. Forming a V-shaped wedge pointing south and taking up a large portion of the park is a Permian marine limestone reef. Laid down in shallow coastal waters 280 to 290 million years ago, it is identified as one of the largest exposed fossil reefs in the world. At the point of the "V" is El Capitan, a sheer, thousand-foot cliff visible for over fifty miles. Nearby is the highest point in Texas, 8,751-foot Guadalupe Peak. Just inside the V-shaped highlands, and a part of McKittrick Canyon, is The Bowl, a 670-acre relict forest con-

Left: *The Guadalupe Mountains thrust upwards from the Texas plain. El Capitan's white face is in center.* Above: *An old but sturdy ranchhouse stands among hardwoods in McKittrick Canyon. Few pioneers lived here because of the steepness of the canyon walls and the lack of space on the canyon floors.*

taining dense stands of ponderosa pine, limber pine and Douglas fir with a thick undergrowth. This small forest is very sensitive to environmental changes.

Archeological and historical remains document man's past activities in the region. Ancient cooking pits attest to the habitation of prehistoric peoples, and in the eastern part of the park are the ruins of Butterfield Stage station, which was a part of the famous Pony Express that preceded the railroads.

Climatic differences at Guadalupe are remarkable. Summer temperatures may be exceedingly hot at lower elevations while the mountain fastnesses are deliciously cool. Fierce summer thunderstorms often cause destructive flash floods, and in autumn, McKittrick Canyon is beautifully colored with the varied tints of its hardwood foliage.

The main road from Carlsbad to El Paso offers scenic views of Guadalupe Peak and El Capitan, but as of early 1972 most of the park is still closed to the visiting public, awaiting implementation of a master plan for park users. However, there is a primitive campground at Pine Springs. Currently, the entrance to McKittrick Canyon is gained only by permission of the park service. In future years, active visitors will be able to experience sights that have long been hidden on this verdant coniferous plateau and in its deep and rugged canyons.

213

Above: *Mount Shuksan thrusts its 9,038-foot height above the autumn foliage at Picture Lake.* Opposite: *Thin clouds stream around Mount Shuksan's peak as seen from a cold, rocky alpine lake at Artist Point.*

NORTH CASCADES

LOCATION: Northwestern Washington
SIZE: 505,000 acres
ESTABLISHED: 1968

Warm breath freezes in the wet coldness of the dark morning, as the mountains await the sun's heat. From the east, the first rays of the coming day edge over the vast land forms, and one by one the dawn's fingers touch the great peaks, illuminating their snow with a pink, then orange, and finally white light. The mists on the upper peaks begin to break and slowly dissipate, and the full majesty of these mountains comes into full view.

To hike these valleys and climb the peaks is one of the most rewarding mountaineering adventures in North America. Montana's Glacier National Park and the Grand Tetons of Wyoming have their glories, but the vast rock cathedrals of Washington's northern Cascades have a scope and grandeur all their own.

Sometimes called the American Alps, these peaks, valleys and lakes sculpted by huge glaciers are con-

The Challenger Glacier on Mount Challenger has many dangerous but beautiful ice crevasses.

sidered by many outdoorsmen to be the most scenic mountain wilderness in the conterminous U. S.

The Cascade Range stretches from British Columbia to northern California, but the North Cascades in Washington contain more spectacular scenery than any other section. Geologically, this mountain range has an unusual history. The first, or "dawn" Cascades, rose from the sea and were completely eroded away within a time span of eons. Then the ocean reflooded the area until about fifteen million years ago when earth convulsions raised the land once again. Erosion stripped these new mountains of their ocean sediment and about one million years ago, more earth movements broke the Cascades along fault lines and lifted the mountains even higher. Then vast ice fields reshaped the land again as three, possibly four, large glacial systems formed in the mountains and moved down the valleys, creating the jagged peaks, U-shaped valleys and sheer cliffs that can be seen today.

The high mountains intercept some of the wettest prevailing Pacific Ocean winds. Their heavy precipitation has produced a region of hanging glaciers, icefalls, ice caps, hanging valleys, waterfalls and alpine lakes nestled in glacial cirques. There are about 318 glaciers, most of which are stable or slightly retreating, and numerous snowfields within the North Cascades complex, which includes the north and south units of the park and Ross Lake and Lake Chelan national recreation areas — over a thousand square miles of mountain wilderness.

Over 130 alpine lakes dot the landscape and innumerable streams and creeks rush down the mountainsides, forming graceful waterfalls. Lake Chelan near Stehekin occupies a glacial trough exceeding 8,500 feet in depth, one of the deepest gorges on the continent. Fifty-five miles long and one to two miles wide, it has all the features of a Norwegian fjord.

Rain and an average of 516 inches of snow fall on the west side of the Cascades annually for a total of 110 inches of precipitation. On the drier, eastern slopes, however, the precipitation averages only thirty-four inches. The Cascade Range is thus responsible for the semiarid plains of eastern Washington.

Naturally there is extreme variation in plant communities between the moisture-laden west side and the dry east slopes. From western rain forests, the vegetation changes to subalpine conifers, verdant meadows and alpine tundra, and then to eastern pine forests and sunny, dry shrublands. The valleys and mountains below the timberline are covered with dense strands of huge Douglas firs, tall hemlocks and Western red cedars, Engelmann and Sitka spruce, ponderosa and lodgepole pines and silver firs. Mixed with the conifers are many deciduous trees — alders, maples, willows and cottonwoods, among others. In the wet valleys on the western slopes, moss grows so profusely that it hangs from the trees.

The most colorful time of year in the high country is July when fields of red, white and yellow heather tint the slopes, mixing with the showy beargrass, and the yellow blossoms of skunk cabbage adorn the marshes around glacial lakes. Glacier lilies poke through the melting snow, phlox bursts into color in the meadows, and dogwood and choke cherry trees give the lower forests some added spring color. In summer whole fields of ripe blueberries await the wilderness gourmet on the high slopes. Tiny, fragile alpine wildflowers grow from every small bit of soil in the rocky uplands and tundras.

Bounding among these tiny flowers and jumping from rock to rock are numerous mountain goats. Black-tailed and mule deer are also present, along with foxes, black bears and coyotes. Though not plentiful, cougars, or mountain lions, have found parts of this wilderness isolated enough from civilization to live peacefully. Among the smaller animals are snowshoe hares, cottontails, aplodontia (mountain beavers), pikas, marmots, porcupines, weasels, beavers and a number of varieties of mice.

Waterfowl is plentiful with mallards, teals, widgeons, geese and goldeneyes sharing the lakes and ponds. Ptarmigan and grouse scurry through the underbrush, and various kinds of hawks and owls prey on the small animal population. In winter large numbers of bald eagles can be seen along the Skagit River feeding on salmon. The sounds of the Cascades' birdlife is varied with common loons and great blue herons adding their shrill calls to the singing of swallows, chickadees, nuthatches, wrens, robins, thrushes, warblers and sparrows.

Over 340 miles of hiking trails provide access to this scenic wilderness. Trails lead to many of the main vistas, such as mounts Shuksan, Logan and Challenger, the Stehekin and Cascade rivers, Eldorado Peak, Cascade Pass and others. For hikers, numerous backcountry campsites are available, and for boaters, several boat-in campgrounds are maintained on lakes Chelan, Ross and Diablo. There are also some developed, roadside campgrounds in Ross Lake National Recreation Area, and several other camps in surrounding Okanogan and Mount Baker national forests.

State Highway 20 follows the Skagit River into Ross Lake recreation area, which separates the north and south units of the park, and regularly scheduled boat runs are taken between Chelan and Stehekin on Lake Chelan at the southern edge of the complex.

A boat moves across the waters of Diablo Lake, whose setting resembles a Norwegian fjord.

The most dramatic views, looking over thousands of square miles of snow, glaciated wilderness peaks and deep green valleys, are available only to hardy hikers from selected ridge vantage points. Reaching such overlooks is a challenging test for mountain climbers and high trail hikers.

The park presently covers only an area originally recommended by a Government study team in 1963, and some conservationists are still arguing that the park should be enlarged further.

Supreme Court Justice William O. Douglas, who has hiked this region for a long lifetime, has written, "The wilderness of the North Cascades is a national resource of the future, not merely a local commodity, and we need it all, as a nation." This new park of towering, craggy ice mountains, flashing streams and waterfalls, blue alpine lakes, forested valleys, colorful flowers and abundant wildlife is, by any test, one of the crowning gems of the National Park System.

Opposite, top: *Fog fills the valley below Sahale Ridge as sunset colors brighten the western sky, ending another day in the American Alps.* Opposite, bottom: *The back-lighted sun accentuates the moss of a lush rain forest on the Cascades' west slopes. Precipitation in these rain forests averages 110 inches annually.* Above: *A young mule deer grazes in the Cascades' evergreen forests.* Below: *The craggy peaks of the Chilli-wack and Pickets ranges reach above the misty clouds. Mount Redoubt, 8,959 feet high near the Canadian border, is in the foreground. On the right horizon is Mount Rainier, 150 miles away, and to its left is 10,541-ft. Glacier Peak in Mt. Baker National Forest.*

REDWOOD

LOCATION: Northern California
SIZE: 57,094 acres
ESTABLISHED: 1968

Along the coast of northern California stand some of the oldest living things on earth. In this redwood country there are groves of giant trees which were growing during the Golden Age of ancient Greece.

In order to save as many of these groves as possible for posterity, conservationists in 1918 formed the Save-the-Redwoods League and began a campaign for a national park in northern California. Exactly fifty years later, in 1968—after a series of stormy battles—their goal was finally realized. Embracing fifty-seven thousand acres of redwoods, bluffs and beaches, Redwood National Park also includes thirty continuous miles of beautiful California coastline. Within the boundaries are three state parks—Jedediah Smith Redwoods, Del Norte Coast Redwoods and Prairie Creek Redwoods—created earlier through the efforts of the Save-The-Redwoods League. These areas will be transferred to the park service and become integral parts of the new national park.

Once growing the entire length of the Pacific coast from Oregon to the Big Sur peninsula, coast redwoods are now confined to relatively small areas, and some of these last groves are being logged as these words are written. There are also private landholdings within the park itself which will be logged unless they are added to the park; one hopes these areas will also be preserved in the near future to protect the ecology of the fragile watersheds. Conservationists are now trying to save these lands by proposing a 33,000-acre increase to the park, including the spacious Redwood Creek watershed on the southern boundary.

The redwood is a living relict of the past. Redwood fossils have been found in Texas, Pennsylvania, Wyoming and even along the Bering Sea in Alaska. Redwoods once grew in Europe until an ice sheet forced them into the Mediterranean. In central China there are hundreds of what are called Dawn Redwoods, deciduous redwoods that have survived millions of years of floods, fires, droughts and ice.

The coast redwood's scientific name is *Sequoia sempervirens*. Sequoia comes from the Cherokee Indian, Sequoyah, who invented an Indian alphabet and taught his people to read and write; *sempervirens* means evergreen. Its close relative, the Sierra redwood *(Sequoia gigantea),* found in Sequoia and Yosemite national parks, is larger in girth and much older, but *sempervirens* is taller. The foliage of the *gigantea* resembles that of juniper, while the *sempervirens's* foliage is more like hemlock. The bark of the Sierra tree is a bright sienna, while the coast version's bark is a dull chocolate. Curiously *sempervirens's* cones are only one-third the size of its cousin's to the east.

The redwood's reproduction cycle is unique in that it is one of the few coniferous trees that reproduces by sprouting from its own root system. Although seeds germinate, they cannot establish a strong root system fast enough to carry them through the summer drought season. The stump sprout already has a developed root system, however, and will quickly mature when the parent dies.

The park's area can be roughly divided into four main ecosystems. The redwood forest ecosystem is a special plant community adapted to the drainage, soil, relatively moderate temperatures and the abundant rain and fog found here—an annual rainfall of a hundred inches is not uncommon. Dominated by the large coast redwood, this ecosystem has an understory thick with smaller trees and shrubs, including flowering rhododendron, huckleberry, salmonberry and azalea. The forest floor, deep with redwood needles and other natural litter, is often out of sight under a cover of ferns. Where the duff is drier and the

Walking among the towering redwood trees in Jedediah Smith Redwoods State Park is a unique experience.

forest crown more open, acres of the floor are taken over by wildflowers — oxalis, wild iris, purple and yellow violets, white trilliums, and redwood and Olympia lilies.

Numerous streams provide a variation in plant life. Inland forest borders are dry from May through October and consequently have different kinds of vegetation, especially oaks and alders. Along the coast, moisture is so abundant that the redwoods must share the ground with hemlock, spruce, fir and cedar.

Wildlife is plentiful. One of the last surviving Californian herds of Roosevelt elk can be seen in the open meadows or on the coast. Also present are black-tailed deer, squirrels, foxes, bobcats, chipmunks, raccoons, beavers and river otters. Birds include Steller's jays, grouse, pileated woodpeckers, Western robins and various kinds of thrushes. The streams support a large population of salmon and trout.

The north coastal scrub ecosystem takes over as the forest thins on approaches to the cliffs and scoops in the coastline. This narrow strip is influenced by almost constant salty winds, rocky soils and poor drainage. Low-growing trees, woody shrubs and herbaceous plants dominate here.

The marine and shore ecosystem is fairly typical of the Pacific Northwest Coast. Offshore rocks are havens for seabirds, seals and sea lions, and migrating whales are often observed near the coast. Tidepools

Roosevelt elk. are sometimes seen on the coast, a dramatic silhouette against the breaking waves.

The Klamath River winds through a succession of redwood-covered mountain ridges shrouded in fog.

and saltwater and freshwater marshes have abundant animal life, and the sandy beaches and dunes are constantly renewed by the ocean's currents.

The cutover forest is a severely damaged redwood forest ecosystem and represents a drastic and sudden change in the once thriving redwood forest. The effects of heavy logging and subsequent erosion of the land have created new conditions for plant and animal life. In theory, such areas will go through a succession of changes and will result hundreds of years hence in a different redwood forest ecosystem.

Notable individual features of the national park include the Tall Trees area along Redwood Creek where the world's tallest tree, 368 feet high, grows. An easy eight-mile-long trail leads to the Tall Trees from nearby U. S. highway 101.

In Prairie Creek Redwoods State Park, Home Creek has cut through the bluffs, forming Fern Canyon, named for the five-fingered ferns and mosses that grow profusely and cover the canyon's fifty-foot high walls.

Highway 101 is the main route in the national park. Each state park is developed with campgrounds, picnic areas, visitor centers and hiking trails, and campgrounds are also found in adjacent Six Rivers National Forest.

At the signing of the bill authorizing Redwood National Park in 1968, President Lyndon Johnson stated, "The Redwoods will stand because men of vision and courage made their stand, refusing to suffer . . . any greater damage to our environment. . . . I believe this act of establishing a Redwood National Park in California will stand for all time as a monument to the wisdom of our generation."

Lush undergrowth (above) results from the heavy precipitation, as much as a hundred inches a year. Del Norte Coast Redwoods State Park (below) is a beautiful meeting of land and sea.

VOYAGEURS

LOCATION: Northern Minnesota
SIZE: 219,431 acres
AUTHORIZED: 1971

During the eighteenth and early nineteenth centuries when ladies of European society demanded the best North American fur for their clothing, these waters in northern Minnesota rang with the singing of French-Canadian *voyageurs*. Wearing bright caps and leather boots, these rugged adventurers paddled and portaged in their fragile, birchbark canoes thousands of tons of furs and trade goods yearly over the three-thousand-mile waterway extending from Montreal to Fort Chipewyan on Lake Athabaska in what is now upper Alberta. Enroute, over a course that included at least 120 portages, they encountered rapids, waterfalls, storms and other dangers.

Like the whalers of Nantucket and the mountain men of the Rockies, the *voyageurs* are now part of a romantic legend. But unlike the scenes where the whalers and mountain men performed their feats, much of the *voyageurs'* water highway remains largely as they knew it—an immense land of green forests and blue waters.

The movement to create a Voyageurs National Park began in 1891 when the State of Minnesota requested congressional authorization for a national park in the Ontario-Minnesota border wilderness. After many years of controversy, the park service finally recommended the region east of International Falls around the Kabetogama Peninsula, and in January 1971 President Richard M. Nixon signed a bill authorizing the nation's thirty-sixth national park.

The park lies just west of the Boundary Waters Canoe Area and is adjacent to the huge Quetico-Superior wilderness, a joint U. S.-Canadian venture which includes Quetico Provincial Park and Superior National Forest.

Consisting of 139,000 acres of north woods country plus eighty thousand acres of water, the park includes large Kabetogama Lake and parts of Rainy and Namekan lakes.

Four times ice sheets edged down from the north, grinding the land bare, and each time these spectacular forests grew back. This is the northern shield region—a land surface shaped by continental glaciation into a vast system of internal waterways. During the lumbering heyday in the last century, many thousands of acres of virgin pine forests in this region were stripped clean by loggers, but the land is now covered once again with large second-growth pines and firs, tapering spruce, fluttering aspens and white-barked birches. Numerous bogs, sand beaches and cliffs break the unending vista of forest, water and sky. The waters

The extensive waterways in Voyageurs provide a natural habitat for moose and other water-preferring animals, such as beavers and otters, plus numerous water birds.

Dark evergreens stand out against autumn's light-colored deciduous trees along developed Ash River, just outside the southern boundary of the park, which can be seen in the distance.

vary from narrows less than fifty feet wide to lakes several miles across, dotted with wooded islands and accented by rocky promontories.

All of these natural features provide food and shelter for a wide variety of wildlife. Moose may sometimes be seen swimming across the lakes, their large snouts making small wakes in the water. White-tailed deer and black bears are common, as are smaller animals such as minks, otters, bobcats and rabbits. Beavers find a wealth of places for their watery homes, and it is one of the few parts of the country where timber wolves may still be found. Unfortunately, wolverines and pine martens have been virtually pushed out of the region, but the park service plans to reintroduce caribou and increase the moose population. Hawks, golden eagles and a wide variety of songbirds and waterfowl make Voyageurs their home during season, and many stay all year around. The lakes contain large numbers of walleyes, northern pikes, lake trout, smallmouth bass and muskellunge, and the lake sturgeon, a rare and endangered fish, lives in some of the larger lakes.

As visitor-use plans are formulated for this newest national park in the coming years, it will be unique in that the waterways themselves will remain the principal means of visitor transportation. Few roadways will be built, and nearby towns will provide most of the visitor facilities.

One writer has said of the *voyageur,* "His canoe has long since vanished from the northern waters, his red cap is seen no more, a bright spot against the blue of Lake Superior; his sprightly French conversation, punctuated with inimitable gesture, his exaggerated courtesy, his incurable romanticism, his songs and his superstitions are gone." But his land remains, the sky-blue water and north woods forests that he knew, preserved in this park for ours and future generations.

A white-barked birch tree frames the early summer greenery surrounding a beaver pond where the enterprising creatures have built a dam to hold back some of winter's melted snow. Although nearly extinct after the eighteenth and early nineteenth century fur boom, when voyageurs would help carry their pelts to European markets, beavers have increased steadily throughout their range in the United States.